The Art *of* CELEBRATING

The Art *of* CELEBRATING

AKESHI AKINSEYE

FOREWORD BY REBECCA GRINNALS AND KATHRYN ARCE

To my family and the place where it all began—My childhood home, filled with laughter, love, and the rhythm of celebration. Thank you for teaching me the beauty of gathering, the joy of traditions, and the power of connection.

Published by Greenleaf Book Group Press
Austin, Texas
www.gbgpress.com

For ordering information or special discounts for bulk purchases, please contact Greenleaf Book Group at PO Box 91869, Austin, TX 78709, 512.891.6100.

Design and composition by Dami Okuboyejo, By Dami Studios
Cover design by Dami Okuboyejo, By Dami Studios

Publisher's Cataloging-in-Publication data is available.

Print ISBN: 979-8-88645-371-3

eBook ISBN: 979-8-88645-372-0

To offset the number of trees consumed in the printing of our books, Greenleaf donates a portion of the proceeds from each printing to the Arbor Day Foundation. Greenleaf Book Group has replaced over 50,000 trees since 2007.

Printed in China on acid-free paper

25 26 27 28 29 30 31 32

First Edition

CONTENTS

FOREWORD

BY REBECCA GRINNALS AND KATHRYN ARCE
Engage! Summits

Celebration is one of the most profound and universal human experiences. Across cultures, histories, and generations, people have gathered to mark milestones, express gratitude, honor traditions, and create moments of joy that leave lasting imprints on the heart. Whether it's an intimate dinner, a grand wedding, a milestone birthday or anniversary, or a simple toast among friends, the act of celebrating is woven into the fabric of our lives.

Akeshi Akinseye's *The Art of Celebrating: Inspiration and Ideas for Meaningful Gatherings* is a masterclass in crafting gatherings that are not only beautiful but also deeply meaningful. It is a book that goes beyond surface-level aesthetics and logistics to explore the emotional and cultural significance of celebrations. Through an expert blend of storytelling, practical advice, and creative inspiration, Akeshi invites us to reimagine how we approach events—not as obligations or grand performances, but as opportunities to forge connections, honor life's journey, and elevate everyday moments into something extraordinary.

At its core, this book is an invitation to be intentional with the way we celebrate. In a world that often rushes from one milestone to the next, we rarely pause to savor the moments that shape our lives. Too often, celebrations become checklist-driven, guided by societal expectations rather than personal meaning. Akinseye reminds us that true celebration is about depth, not just grandeur. It is about curating experiences that reflect our values, tell our stories, and bring people together in ways that feel authentic and fulfilling.

What makes *The Art of Celebrating* so compelling is its blend of expertise and heartfelt wisdom. As a visionary in the world of event design, Akeshi has cultivated a reputation for creating experiences that are not just visually stunning but emotionally resonant. Her work is a testament to the power of storytelling in event planning—how the smallest details, from the choice of music to the scent of a candle, can evoke memory, emotion, and meaning. In these pages, she generously shares the principles and inspirations behind this approach, offering readers not just a guide, but a philosophy for celebrating life with intention and artistry.

This book is both practical and poetic, offering readers a roadmap for creating unforgettable gatherings. It provides insights into designing events that feel deeply personal, from understanding the psychology of celebration to choosing elements that align with the essence of the occasion. Readers will find inspiration in the rich cultural perspectives woven throughout, learning how different traditions across the world honor milestones and create a sense of belonging.

One of the most powerful aspects of this book is its emphasis on inclusivity and emotional connection. Akeshi reminds us that celebrations should not be about perfection but about presence. She encourages us to move beyond superficial standards of success and instead focus on crafting experiences that make people feel seen, valued, and connected. In a time when digital interactions often replace face-to-face connections, this message is more vital than ever.

For those who plan gatherings professionally, *The Art of Celebrating* offers a fresh perspective on what it means to be an event curator. It is a call to approach event design as an art form—one that combines visual beauty with emotional resonance, logistics with storytelling, and tradition with innovation. For those who simply love hosting, it is an invitation to embrace the joy of bringing people together with authenticity and creativity.

As you turn these pages, prepare to be inspired. You will find yourself rethinking the way you approach celebrations, whether large or small. You will be encouraged to embrace the beauty of everyday moments, to honor traditions in new and meaningful ways, and to craft gatherings that leave a lasting imprint on those who attend.

Akeshi Akinseye has given us a gift with this book—a reminder that life is meant to be celebrated, not just on special occasions, but in the quiet, beautiful moments that make up our days. *The Art of Celebrating* is more than a guide; it is a philosophy, a source of inspiration, and a testament to the power of human connection. May this book inspire you to celebrate more deeply, more intentionally, and with more heart. After all, in the end, the greatest celebrations are not about the grandeur of the occasion, but the depth of the memories created.

INTRODUCTION

Celebrations have always held a special place in my heart. Growing up in Benin City, Nigeria, they weren't just events—they were a way of life. Cooking, entertaining, and hosting were woven into the fabric of our family gatherings. Whether it was a wedding, birthday, or holiday, each celebration brought people together to share in love, connection, and joy. These early experiences shaped how I view the world: Celebrations are expressions of beauty and togetherness, moments that remind us of what truly matters.

Our home was the heart of family gatherings. I still remember the buzz of excitement as relatives arrived—cousins, aunties, uncles, and even hired cooks, with their massive pots and fresh ingredients, ready to prepare for the festivities. Cooking started days in advance, and as kids, my siblings, cousins, and I eagerly helped while sneaking tastes of dishes in progress. These memories are etched in my heart, filled with warmth, laughter, and the unbreakable bond of family.

When I moved to Chicago after high school to study psychology, I thought I wanted to be a therapist. But far from home and family, I found myself drawn to hosting. I would invite friends to my apartment, cook meals, mix cocktails, and create spaces for us to gather. Perhaps it was my way of filling the void I felt being away from home. Celebrating, it seems, is in my core—instilled in me by my mother.

I began renting spaces for dinner parties, rooftop gatherings, and all kinds of celebrations. Encouraged by my mother and friends, I decided to take a leap of faith and launch my own business. Initially, I thought to combine my love for planning and my passion for cooking by starting a catering and planning company. I obtained my catering license, ready to deliver an incredible experience to my clients through food, entertaining, and planning.

Although I love to cook, I quickly realized that catering was a demanding endeavor, instilling in me a respect and admiration for professional caterers. It was challenging, and I knew changes were necessary. I'm grateful to the clients who trusted me with their events—I even catered a few weddings, including my own! Eventually, my husband and I decided to pivot, focusing solely on wedding and event planning. However, I felt something crucial was still missing: design.

While my background in helping my mom during my childhood had given me some design experience, I knew nothing about working with fresh flowers, which I was eager to learn. I decided to fully immerse myself in the world of floral design, attending workshops, purchasing classes, and scouring the internet for tips and tricks. It was a terrifying leap into the unknown, but it paid off tremendously. I'm thrilled I took that step, as it allowed me to offer the full experience of planning and design to my clients.

That leap led me to launch Kesh Events, taking me on an incredible journey from planning my own personal gatherings to designing bespoke celebrations for discerning clients around the world. Today, I'm fortunate to plan and design all manner of events, from baby showers and engagement parties to milestone birthdays and luxury weddings. For me, each celebration is an opportunity to bring people together in a meaningful way, honor their connections, create beauty, and craft unforgettable memories.

A few years after launching Kesh Events, I felt the urge to extend my love for celebrations beyond event planning. This passion led me to create *The Art of Celebrating*—a lifestyle, entertaining, design, and celebrations blog that combines expert insights with creative inspiration for elegant living. Covering everything from hosting and party planning to seasonal recipes, home décor, travel, and style, it became a space to share my love for curating experiences that elevate life's most meaningful moments with beauty and intention.

Shortly after, *The Art of Celebrating* magazine followed, delivering quarterly digital editions filled with inspiration to help readers craft unforgettable celebrations.

This expansion allowed me to merge my expertise in event planning with my passion for storytelling, offering readers insider knowledge, creative tips, and expert advice on how to celebrate life beautifully.

Through both the blog and magazine, I've been able to connect with a community of hosts, creatives, and design enthusiasts who, like me, believe in the power of celebrating with intention. Whether sharing expert advice, curating seasonal trends, or offering creative resources, my mission has remained the same—to help others create celebrations that are not only visually stunning but also personal and meaningful.

In a world that moves so quickly, celebrations offer us a rare and precious chance to pause and embrace the people and moments around us. They allow us to step away from the noise, be present with the people we care about, and embrace the beauty of the moment.

My love for celebrations was nurtured by my mother, who was the heartbeat of our family's gatherings. She approached every event with joy and pride, designing, cooking, and hosting with intention and care, and I carry that same sense of joy and pride with me today in my work and when I host. It's through her that I learned the art of celebrating, and those lessons have stayed with me, shaping my career as a wedding/event planner, designer, and entrepreneur.

Celebrations are a canvas for storytelling, a chance to honor the connections that bring us together. The smallest details—the texture of a napkin, the flavor of a signature drink, or the placement of a centerpiece—can elevate a gathering from routine to remarkable. Thoughtfulness and care remind our guests that they are seen, valued, and celebrated. Embracing the art of celebrating is an art in itself. It's allowing yourself to open your heart to meaningful experience and connection, tapping into your creative side and planning with intention.

This book is a reflection of everything I've learned—from the vibrant traditions of my childhood to my experiences planning and designing events around the world. Inside this book, I share personal experiences from my journey as a planner and designer and help you find the confidence to host in style. Whether you're hosting an intimate dinner or a grand celebration, the heart of every event remains the same: creating spaces for people to connect, share, and celebrate something meaningful.

With practical tips, creative ideas, and inspiration drawn from my journey, I hope this book empowers you to approach your celebrations with intentionality and reverence. After all, the moments we take the time to cherish are the ones we carry with us forever. Join me on this journey, and together, let's make every moment worth celebrating.

Pavel

CHAPTER 01

FINDING INSPIRATION

Setting the Foundation for Your Celebration.

Inspiration plays a pivotal role in creating memorable celebrations. It sets the tone, colors, texture, and vibe of the event, transforming ordinary moments into extraordinary experiences. Whether it's a grand wedding, an intimate dinner party, or a festive holiday gathering, inspiration is the spark that ignites creativity and guides the planning process.

FINDING INSPIRATION IN THEMES

Themes are essential for setting the mood and creating a cohesive experience for your celebration. They provide a sense of direction for everything, from decor and food to invitations and entertainment. A well-chosen theme ties all the details together, creating a seamless flow and atmosphere that guests can fully immerse themselves in.

Themes also give your celebration a purpose; whether it's a birthday, holiday, or just an excuse to gather, they add a layer of fun and intention to the event.

In my work, understanding the theme or vibe my clients envision is crucial. Whether they prefer something formal, playful, colorful, or laid-back, my approach involves diving deep into their inspirations. I often start by assigning a simple yet revealing task: Create a gallery of inspiring images, from fabrics and fashion to food and architecture. This exercise is not only enjoyable but also illuminative, as it often uncovers a common theme in their collection, even when clients initially struggle to articulate their preferences. This method ensures that every celebration reflects a deep, personal connection to the themes that inspire them.

Setting the Foundation for Your Celebration

CONSIDER THE SEASON AS YOU CHOOSE YOUR THEME.

SEASONAL THEMES

Seasonal themes are a powerful way to anchor your celebration's atmosphere, offering unique elements that enhance ambiance, decor, and even the menu. For example, in planning a fall wedding, I've embraced the season's rich palette—browns, golds, oranges, and reds—and incorporated natural elements like pumpkin centerpieces and wooden decor. Seasonal spices and flavors are threaded through each course, from cinnamon garnishes in drinks to warm, spiced entrees.

In spring, I create lush garden party themes using the abundance of flowers and soft pastels, crafting a blooming, fresh setting that brings the outdoors inside. For winter celebrations, I love to design a winter wonderland theme, with white and silver elements and cozy signatures like plush fabrics on chairs and crystal decorations, all under the glow of twinkling lights.

These examples show how tapping into the essence of each season can inspire your theme choice and ensure your celebration is not only timely but also resonant and memorable. Drawing from natural color palettes, seasonal flavors, or the general mood of the time of year helps create an immersive experience for your guests.

BREAKING DOWN INSPIRATION

When considering your inspiration for a celebration, break it down into key elements to ensure a cohesive and well-thought-out event.

- **Colors**: Choose a color palette that reflects the mood and theme of your event. Consider seasonal colors or those that evoke the desired emotions.
- **Scents**: Fragrances can significantly enhance the ambiance. Think about incorporating scents through flowers, candles, or even the food and drinks being served.
- **Mood**: Decide on the overall mood you want to create—whether it's romantic, festive, elegant, or casual.
- **Music style:** Select music that complements the theme and mood of your event. Music can transform the atmosphere and keep guests engaged.
- **Setting/location:** The location of your event will influence many aspects of the planning process. Consider the season and weather when deciding on an indoor or outdoor setting.

DESIGNING THE GUEST EXPERIENCE

At its core, the purpose of throwing a celebration is to create a meaningful and positive experience for your guests. It's important to remember that, while planning can be thrilling, the ultimate goal is how your guests feel throughout the event. Every decision, from the decor to the food and music, should be made with their experience in mind. Consider every aspect of their journey—how they are greeted, the ambiance as they step into the space, and the memories they'll carry with them afterward.

One of the critical elements of the guest experience is the entrance, which sets the tone for the event. I take particular pride in designing grand entrances—an aspect I'm known for. For large-scale celebrations, I meticulously plan the space to include dramatic floral arrangements, striking drapery, or both, often enhancing staircases and doorways with unexpected and beautiful adornments.

For more intimate gatherings, a grand centerpiece or elegant candles might suffice. Sometimes, the most memorable first impression isn't decor—it could be an experiential element, such as welcome drinks, or immersive entertainment, like fire dancers or a solo singer, tailored to the theme. I encourage creativity in this area; for instance, at one event, we arranged for a bartender with a champagne-filled bar cart inside the elevator, ensuring guests were greeted with a sparkling surprise as soon as they stepped inside.

So you see, creating a memorable guest experience means thinking through every touchpoint, from the moment your guests receive the invitation to the final farewell at the end of the evening. Designing this experience goes beyond decor and entertainment; it's about how your guests feel throughout the event.

Mini Lobster Roll
On Buttery Brioche Roll

Elements of a Great Guest Experience

- **Arrival:** Think about how your guests will feel upon arriving. Will there be a welcome drink, decor, coat check, an escort to their seats, or special entertainment to create an immediate impression?
- **Flow of the event:** Consider how the event will move from one moment to the next. Will there be a cocktail hour followed by dinner? Is there enough time between courses for mingling? What happens after dinner and dancing? Will there be an after-party? The goal is to create a flow that makes sense and takes your guest on a journey.
- **Personalization:** Add small, thoughtful details that show you've considered your guests' comfort and enjoyment. Personalized place cards, tailored favors, and thoughtful touches can elevate the experience.
- **Entertainment:** Ensure your entertainment reflects the vibe of the event and keeps your guests engaged. Whether it's a live band, DJ, or interactive elements like a strolling musician or fire dancers, make sure the entertainment aligns with the tone of your celebration.

EVENT CONSIDERATIONS

- **Plated versus stationed food:** Decide if you want a formal sit-down meal or more casual food stations. Each style offers a different dining experience.
- **Formal or casual:** Determine the level of formality for your event. This will guide decisions on dress code, decor, and overall vibe.
- **Size of the party:** The number of guests will affect your planning, from venue size to catering needs.
- **Location:** The venue should align with your theme and accommodate your guest list comfortably.
- **Time of day:** Whether your event is held in the daytime or the evening will influence the lighting, food, and activities you plan.

Timing: Daytime versus Evening

The time of day can significantly influence the feel and structure of your event. A daytime garden party will have a very different ambiance than an elegant evening affair. Consider the lighting, meal options, and guest attire when planning for the time of day.

Think of these considerations as the foundation of your event. Once you have a clear vision, your imagination will begin to run wild with creative ideas.

DAYTIME EVENT TIPS

- Choose lighter, brighter colors for decor and more casual attire for guests.
- Opt for a lighter menu, with seasonal ingredients.
- Plan activities that take advantage of natural light and outdoor settings.

EVENING EVENT TIPS

- Go for richer colors, dramatic lighting, and a more formal dress code.
- Consider a more robust menu, with heavier entrées and signature cocktails.
- Plan entertainment like live music or dancing to keep the energy high throughout the evening.

Digital Mood Board

Create a digital collage that includes photos, color swatches, and other visual elements that reflect your theme. For example, if you're planning a summer garden party, your board might include floral arrangements, color schemes, table settings, and even dress codes that align with the season.

Mood boards allow you to visualize your event as a whole, ensuring that every element—from decor to table settings—feels cohesive and aligned with your vision. They serve as a constant reminder of your inspiration, helping you stay aligned with your vision as you make decisions about design and execution. Whether you choose a digital or physical board, mood boards are a powerful way to keep your event cohesive, creative, and perfectly curated.

CREATING MOOD BOARDS

A mood board is an invaluable tool for visualizing your inspiration and bringing your ideas to life. It's a creative road map that helps you curate the look, feel, and overall atmosphere of your celebration. Here's how to create one:

Physical Mood Board

Collect fabrics, magazine pages, photos, and other tangible items that inspire you. Arrange these elements on a physical board to see how they come together. Feel free to play around with placement to see how these different elements interact. This process can spark new ideas and give you a deeper sense of how your event will come together visually.

PERSONAL SOURCES OF INSPIRATION

Growing up, my mother's kitchen was a hub of creativity. The aromas, colors, and flavors from her cooking often serve as my inspiration. I remember the joy and pride she put into every meal and how these meals became the centerpiece of our family gatherings. These memories inspire many of the culinary themes in my events today.

Another significant source of inspiration was my mother's tailoring shop. I found the fabrics fascinating—their colors, textures, and patterns sparked my imagination. Watching my mother transform these fabrics into beautiful garments taught me the importance of detail and craftsmanship, lessons that I carry into my event designs today.

My travels also serve as a major source of inspiration. Experiencing different cultures, cuisines, and traditions has enriched my creative palette.

From savoring the incredible cuisine in Thailand and exploring the picturesque landscapes of Paris, to soaking in the serene vistas of Lake Como and admiring the intricate tile designs and fabrics in Marrakech, each destination I visit adds a new layer of inspiration into my work. I'm continually inspired by the bursts of beauty that surround me during my travels. I encourage you to think about your own personal experiences and what inspires you. Perhaps it's the cultural traditions you grew up with, the places you've traveled to, or even the scenery right outside your window. Your unique background and experiences can add personal, meaningful touches to your celebrations.

By incorporating these elements, you'll create an event that feels deeply personal and resonates with both you and your guests.

BUILDING THE TIMELINE AND CHECKLIST

Once the theme and tone are set, it's time to break down the planning process into manageable steps. Creating a detailed timeline and checklist are your best tools for staying organized and on track. A well-thought-out timeline ensures that you have ample time for each task and can focus on the details without feeling rushed.

FOUR-WEEK TIMELINE FOR PLANNING AN INTIMATE DINNER PARTY

Four Weeks Before:

1. **Set the date and guest list:** Finalize the date and list of attendees (six to ten guests is ideal for an intimate gathering).
2. **Select the theme:** Decide on a theme or mood (e.g., cozy, elegant, or seasonal), and choose a color palette for the table.
3. **Plan the menu:** Design a well-rounded menu with appetizers, a main course, sides, and dessert. Consider dietary preferences.
4. **Create a budget:** Allocate funds for food, drinks, decor, and any extras, like entertainment, lighting, rentals, staffing, etc.
5. **Send invitations:** Send digital or printed invitations to confirm the availability of guests.

“

BY BREAKING TASKS INTO SMALLER, MANAGEABLE STEPS OVER THE COURSE OF FOUR WEEKS, YOU CAN ENJOY HOSTING YOUR DINNER PARTY WITH EASE AND CONFIDENCE.

LIVE BEAUTIFUL
The Art of Home
Architects on Architecture
THE STYLISH LIFE
at 100

Three Weeks Before:

1. **Design the tablescape:** Decide on table settings, centerpieces, linens, and place cards.
2. **Plan drinks:** Select a signature cocktail or mocktail, wine pairings, and nonalcoholic options.
3. **Test recipes:** Try out any unfamiliar recipes to perfect them ahead of time.
4. **Order specialty items:** Purchase or preorder items like unique ingredients, floral arrangements, or candles.
5. **Draft a timeline:** Create a detailed schedule for the evening and plan out key moments like cocktails, dinner, and dessert.

Two Weeks Before:

1. **Confirm RSVPs:** Follow up with guests who haven't responded.
2. **Shop for nonperishables:** Purchase pantry items, wines, spirits, and decor items that won't spoil.
3. **Review tableware:** Ensure you have enough plates, glasses, utensils, and napkins.
4. **Arrange seating:** Plan the seating chart to create a warm, inviting atmosphere.
5. **Plan ambient details:** Choose background music, lighting, and any additional touches to enhance the mood.

One Week Before:

1. **Clean and organize:** Tidy up the event space and clear any clutter.
2. **Plan your perishables:** Make a detailed list of perishable items—like produce, proteins, and dairy—to buy a day or two before the event.
3. **Confirm final details:** Follow up with vendors such as florists, bakers, or rental companies to reconfirm delivery and setup times.
4. **Pre-set your table:** If possible, test and style your tablescape ahead of time to ensure all elements are cohesive and complete.

Two to Three Days Before:

1. **Do the main shopping:** Purchase fresh ingredients and beverages.
2. **Prepare decor:** Prep your florals, iron linens, and finalize table details.
3. **Prep ingredients:** Chop vegetables, marinate proteins, and premeasure dry ingredients.
4. **Chill beverages:** Place wines and other drinks in the fridge to chill.
5. **Confirm timeline:** Review the schedule to ensure the flow of the evening works seamlessly.

The Day Before:

1. **Send reminder messages:** A few days before the event, send a reminder to your guests reconfirming essential details such as the start time, dress code, and parking information. This helps ensure that everyone is well informed and can plan accordingly.
2. **Express your excitement:** In your communications, express your enthusiasm about hosting the event. A personal touch in your message can make your guests feel genuinely welcome and eager to join the celebration.
3. **Set the table ahead of time:** Arrange your table settings well before your guests arrive. This not only helps you avoid last-minute stress but also allows you to pay attention to the finer details of presentation, ensuring everything looks perfect as soon as your guests walk in.

The Day of Event:

1. **Cook early:** Prepare dishes that can be made ahead of time, leaving only final touches or warming up for later.
2. **Set the mood:** Arrange flowers, adjust lighting, and start the playlist an hour before guests arrive.
3. **Finish setup:** Lay out final place settings, double-check the seating chart, and set up the bar or drink station.
4. **Freshen up:** Take thirty minutes to relax and get dressed before the party begins.
5. **Welcome guests:** Greet each guest warmly and guide them to cocktails or appetizers.

Tips for Your Event Planning Timeline:

1. **Start early:** For larger events like weddings, start planning at least twelve to eighteen months in advance. For smaller gatherings, aim for a three-to-sixmonth window. For intimate dinner parties, a fourweek window allows you to thoughtfully curate every detail without feeling rushed.
2. **Create a detailed checklist:** Break down tasks by category, such as venue selection, decor, food, entertainment, and guest management. Within each category, list specific tasks and deadlines.
3. **Prioritize:** Focus on securing major elements first, like the venue, caterer, and entertainment. Once those key components are locked in, you can shift to the finer details.
4. **Keep track of your budget:** Allocate funds for each aspect of the event and track spending as you go. Having a clear budget in place will prevent overspending and keep your vision grounded in reality.

PLAN WITH PURPOSE

Planning a celebration is more than just managing logistics; it's about creating a meaningful experience that leaves a lasting impression on your guests and forms cherished memories for you, the host. For me, the excitement begins the moment I start dreaming up an event and holds constant throughout the entirety of the planning and event itself. But once the initial thrill subsides, I always ask myself the most important question: Why am I hosting this? What's the reason for the celebration?

From there, I focus on curating the guest experience. What do I want them to feel? How do I want them to engage with the event? These questions guide every decision, shaping the flow, decor, and overall atmosphere. They say love is in the details, and I couldn't agree more. The more thought and intention you put into the small elements—whether the layout of the space or a personalized touch for each guest—the more impactful your celebration becomes.

Remember, every great event begins with a clear vision and careful planning. When you lay the right foundation, you'll be able to bring your ideas to life and create an unforgettable experience for your guests.

BRINGING IT ALL TOGETHER

Once you've gathered your inspiration, it's time to build on it. Decide on a theme that reflects the mood and experience you want to create. Choose colors that complement your theme and evoke the desired emotions. Consider the textures and tones that will enhance the overall vibe of your celebration.

Remember, inspiration is not just about the big picture; it's also about the small details that make your event unique. From the invitations to the table settings, every element should reflect the inspired vision you've created.

In the following chapters, we'll explore how to turn your inspiration into reality, with practical tips and ideas for planning and executing unforgettable celebrations. But for now, let your imagination run wild, and embrace the beauty of inspiration.

LAYING THE GROUNDWORK FOR AN INTENTIONAL CELEBRATION

Before diving into planning, reflect on the bigger picture —how you want the celebration to feel, flow, and unfold. Use these prompts and strategies to shape a meaningful and beautifully cohesive event:

- **Start with a theme:** Choose a concept or mood that reflects the purpose of your gathering. Let it guide every decision—from florals to food to entertainment.
- **Create a visual guide:** Build a mood board (digital or physical) to explore color palettes, textures, and tones. This becomes your creative anchor.
- **Think seasonally:** Use the time of year to influence your palette, ingredients, and atmosphere—enhancing authenticity and relevance.
- **Design with purpose:** Map out the guest experience from the moment they arrive. What will they see, hear, feel, and taste? Prioritize comfort, joy, and flow.
- **Prioritize early planning:** Secure high-impact vendors—venue, catering, design—before diving into details. This gives you more freedom and flexibility as you build.

CHAPTER 02

CREATING MEMORABLE MOMENTS

Adding Personal Touches.

When planning a celebration, whether it's a grand affair or an intimate gathering, personal touches and meaningful details are what turn it into something really unforgettable. The best celebrations are not only beautiful but also deeply personal, filled with elements that resonate with you and your guests. These moments are what linger in people's hearts long after the party.

I've always believed that one of the keys to any memorable event lies in those special, unique touches that reflect the personality and story of the host. It's the thoughtfulness behind the details—the small things that show you've truly considered your guests—that transforms a gathering from ordinary to extraordinary. That's why I encourage you to think about these personal elements early in the planning process, before getting caught up in the logistics and other details.

Adding Personal Touches

Signature Drinks
His
Hers
Tequila
Fresh Lime Juice
Tabasco
Ours
Agave
Jus De Citron Vert
Cordial D'argumes
Fentimans
Pink Grapefruit Tonic Water

We love to personalize signature drinks and mocktails by giving them fun, meaningful names that reflect the couple or milestone celebration. Another way to add personalization is through the actual selection of drinks at the bar. Rather than choosing generic cocktails, we curate the menu based on the couple's personal tastes. If the groom is a tequila lover, for example, we'll craft a signature cocktail featuring tequila as the star ingredient. These details not only make the bar experience more unique but also create a deeper connection between the celebration and the couple's story.

In this chapter, we'll focus on setting the emotional tone of your event and the importance of personalization. Whether it's through a thoughtfully crafted invitation, a signature cocktail inspired by a special memory, or a carefully selected playlist that brings back fond memories, the personal details are what truly make an event your own.

START WITH EMOTION

Before diving into the "what" and "how" of planning, I always ask my clients, "How do you want your guests to feel?" This should guide every decision. Whether you want your guests to feel relaxed, joyful, nostalgic, or inspired, setting an emotional tone early will help shape everything else—from decor and music to food and flow.

Think about past celebrations that meant something to you. What made them stand out? Was it the warmth of the setting, the laughter around the dinner table, or the joy of reconnecting with old friends? These emotions should guide your decisions as you design your event.

MAKING A GOOD FIRST IMPRESSION: SETTING THE TONE

A great celebration begins the moment guests arrive, and a well-thought-out first impression can set a welcoming and exciting tone for the entire event. I love to begin every celebration with a welcome sign that not only stands alone but is adorned with flowers, a solo musician, or a string trio. Imagine this: A refreshing welcome drink is handed to guests as they enter, creating an immediate sense of hospitality, which is soon followed by lively entertainment—perhaps a live musician or upbeat playlist—a personalized welcome sign, and a stunning statement decor piece, like an elaborate floral arrangement or flowers in unexpected areas like the doorway or even the stairway. Now you've successfully crafted an entry that resonates and makes an impact.

The opening moments of any event should make guests feel valued and give them a taste of the experience ahead. Setting the tone from the very start encourages your guests to relax, engage, and fully embrace the celebration.

PERSONALIZATION

The personal touches you incorporate will make your celebration memorable and unique to you and your guests. From the color palette to the choice of flowers, entertainment, or the design of the table settings, every detail can tell a story. Personalization is the beautiful balance between honoring your own style and creating thoughtful moments for your guests. You want your celebration to be unique to you and the reason for the celebration, but you also want to keep what matters to your guests in mind. Often, it's the smallest gestures that leave the greatest impression, showing your guests that you were truly thinking of them.

THE MOST MEANINGFUL MOMENTS ARE BORN FROM THE SMALLEST PERSONAL DETAILS.

For my clients, I always love weaving in elements from their personal lives—whether it's a nod to their heritage, a favorite dish, a song that holds sentimental value, or a place they cherish. I start with the client and do some digging to really get to know them and what matters to them; in the planning process, my job is to find ways to infuse those things in a meaningful and impactful way. The next phase of our planning is focused on the guests and how we can make them get lost in the beautiful details that are curated for them—surprises and all.

These intentional and personal touches make guests feel included in something special, and they carry that with them.

THE SMALLEST TOUCHES—LIKE A NAME ON A MENU—CAN LEAVE THE BIGGEST IMPRESSIONS.

At another event, the guest names were embroidered on the dinner napkins. It was an unexpected and impactful treat for the guests. No detail is too small to consider, so take your time thinking of ways to personalize the celebration and experience. These small details show care and thoughtfulness and can spark conversations and fond memories.

Another meaningful way to add personal touches is through the design of your menu. Imagine incorporating flavors that remind you of your childhood or a favorite dish that you and your partner shared from your travels or even your engagement. Speaking of the menu, an impactful way to tie in personalized touches at your celebrations, no matter the size, is adding each guest name to the menu card. At one of my celebrations we planned, we surprised guests with their names printed on standing acrylic menus. The menus and stationery for the event were designed by my dear friend and creative partner, Dami, owner of **By Dami Studios.** It was a hit, and guests were excited to take their menus home with them. It was a lovely surprise and delight.

As part of our planning process, we always opt for a custom crest or monogram that can be thoughtfully incorporated throughout the celebration—starting with the save-the-dates and invitations. But the real magic happens on the day of the event. A well-placed monogram or crest adds a refined, personal touch to welcome signs, cocktail stirrers, napkins, menus, and even embroidered dinner linens. The key is striking the right balance—too much can feel overdone, but when used intentionally, it's an exquisite detail that elevates the entire celebration.

Ring for Champagne
Ring for Champagne

A

The cocktail napkin doesn't always need a monogram or logo. It's a fun opportunity to get creative. For clients, we've included fun facts about them—an engaging conversation starter for guests. Tying in personal details can make a memorable impact. We've even used monograms, quotes, or playful wording on bathroom hand towels to extend the experience.

Sip and Repeat
Because no great dinner
party ever started
with someone eating a salad
Grab a Drink
Here are Akeshi's favorites
FRENCH MARTINI with a twist
Vodka, Pineapple, Raspberry
OLD FASHIONED with a twist
Bourbon, Schlitz Demerara, Bitters

BUILDING IN MEMORIES EARLY

It's easy to get swept up in the practicalities of planning — choosing vendors, setting budgets, and managing RSVPs—but don't let these tasks overshadow the real purpose of your celebration. By building in these meaningful, personal elements early on, you set the right foundation for an event that will leave a lasting impact.

You also want to consider how you want your guests to interact and engage throughout the event. Will there be a moment for reflection? A way to honor the special people in your life? Giving this consideration from the start makes it easier to find natural ways to weave them into the event rather than tacking them on at the end. Incorporating toasts from those closest to you is a good way to tie in emotion. Make sure the toasts are not too long and there aren't too many.

Whether it's a handwritten note on each place setting, a special toast, or even a surprise element that's revealed during the event, these thoughtful touches are what turn moments into memories. And when guests leave your celebration, it's not the perfectly placed flowers or the impeccable timing they'll remember—it's the emotion, the personal connections, and the sense of being part of something special.

SURPRISE AND DELIGHT: CREATING UNFORGETTABLE MOMENTS

Elevate your event by finding small, thoughtful ways to surprise and delight your guests. Personal touches like having each guest's name on their menu or napkin make them feel truly valued. Unexpected entertainment, such as a surprise performance between courses, keeps the energy fresh and engaging. And when it comes to dessert, think beyond the standard; miniature cakes, tableside toppings, or interactive dessert stations bring a playful twist to the experience. For outdoor celebrations on hot summer days, we have curated popsicle and ice cream stations, which guests loved and appreciated.

Another memorable surprise we curated was for a wedding's welcome celebration in Paris. To give guests an immersive experience, we incorporated surprise entertainment and cabaret performances throughout the evening — an elegant nod to the vibrant spirit of the city. The energy was infectious, and guests were captivated, making it the perfect introduction to the magic of Paris.

As you plan your next gathering, think beyond the expected. Use these moments to dream big and craft experiences that make your celebration truly unforgettable and unique.

THOUGHTFUL HOSTING GOES BEYOND DECOR AND DINING—IT'S ABOUT ANTICIPATING YOUR GUESTS' NEEDS AND ENSURING THEY FEEL WELCOMED, COMFORTABLE, AND CARED FOR THROUGHOUT THE EVENT.

THOUGHTFUL CONSIDERATIONS: KEEPING THE GUESTS' COMFORT IN MIND

From bathroom amenities and personalized seating arrangements to shade solutions for outdoor gatherings, small yet meaningful touches create an atmosphere where guests can relax, engage, and fully enjoy the celebration.

Bathroom Amenities

Having great food and drinks is essential, but a truly memorable event requires attention to every little detail—whether it's a wedding, dinner party, or even a casual girls' night. A good host always thinks beyond the basics, considering elements that ensure guests feel comfortable and cared for.

For instance, we always ensure the restrooms or bathrooms at an event are thoughtfully stocked for guests. Instead of traditional cloth hand towels, I strongly recommend using lovely disposable hand towels, both for hygiene and convenience.

Additionally, we like to provide bathroom amenities along with fun signage that outlines the emergency items available for guests, such as mints, hair supplies, sanitary items, a small first-aid kit, and more. These thoughtful additions ensure that if a guest has a minor mishap, they're covered, without feeling uncomfortable or having to ask for assistance.

Keep in mind that the bathroom's ambiance matters, too. Create an inviting atmosphere by using scented candles or diffuser sticks to keep the space smelling fresh and welcoming, along with some flowers. And don't forget the practicalities—ensure there's a good stock of toiletries so your guests never feel caught off guard. By paying attention to these small yet meaningful details, you elevate the guest experience and leave a lasting impression of care and thoughtfulness.

Seating Arrangements: Thoughtful Touches for Comfort and Ease

When it comes to personalization, I think about every detail, right down to the seating arrangement and style. For intimate dinner parties, a formal seating chart or escort card display may not be necessary, but it's still important to guide guests to their seats if they are assigned. As the host, take the time to direct people to their places—it avoids the awkwardness of wandering around the table looking for where to sit. Adding personalized place cards at each setting is a simple but impactful touch that guests appreciate.

For larger gatherings, such as weddings or more formal events, a seating assignment display becomes essential. Whether it's a seating chart on a board, a mirror with calligraphy, a creative wall display, or a classic escort card table adorned with flowers, ensure it's both visible and clear. While I adore a timeless paper escort card, I also love thinking outside the box and exploring creative displays that add personality to the celebration.

Whatever style you choose, be intentional about making it easy for your guests to find their seats. Clear and thoughtful seating arrangements not only keep the event organized but also add an extra layer of elegance and care to the guest experience.

A

Fun in the Sun: Prioritize Shade and Guest Comfort

For celebrations like pool parties or outdoor events, guest comfort is key. Think of ways to elevate their experience with thoughtful accessories, like sunglasses, scarves, hats for both ladies and gents, and even sunscreen. A few years ago, we planned a multi-day birthday celebration in Mexico, and one of the days featured a pool party. Pool parties in Mexico are always a good idea, but what made this one stand out was the setup we created for guest comfort. We included a station, with fun signage, offering hats for men and women, sunglasses, scarves, sunscreen, lip balm, and towels for the beach. It was a total hit—guests loved the attention to detail and felt cared for.

Providing adequate shade is a crucial element in planning outdoor events. For that birthday soiree and pool party, we ensured guests had comfortable spaces to relax by setting up cabanas and daybeds with umbrellas—allowing them to enjoy the festivities without worrying about the heat. The last thing you want is for guests to feel uncomfortable or overheated.

For weddings and outdoor cocktail receptions, shaded seating areas or strategically placed umbrellas are a must. Thinking ahead and anticipating your guests' needs ensures they can fully enjoy the celebration. No one wants to spend too much time in the scorching sun—comfort and experience should always go hand in hand.

Hydration is also essential. Greet guests with refreshing welcome drinks and set up water stations to keep everyone cool. For weddings and cocktail receptions, I love getting creative with fun additions, like fan programs that double as keepsakes or cool treats such as ice cream and popsicle stations. These thoughtful details not only keep guests comfortable but also add a layer of charm and fun to the event.

Seating is another key element that often gets overlooked but makes a significant impact on guest comfort. Guests—especially those in high heels—will appreciate designated areas where they can take a break and enjoy the moment. Whether it's shaded lounge groupings, cozy seating nooks, or strategically placed benches throughout the venue, providing comfortable spaces for guests to rest ensures they feel cared for throughout the celebration. Thoughtful details like these not only enhance the guest experience but also leave a lasting impression, making your event both stylish and welcoming.

Lounge Groupings: Creating Cozy Spaces for Connection

Lounge groupings are a stylish and thoughtful way to create fun, cozy areas for your guests to sit, mingle, and relax. Whether it's during the cocktail hour, after dinner, or for an after-party, these seating arrangements encourage conversation and connection while adding a layer of sophistication to your event.

I love incorporating lounge groupings around the dance floor if space allows. It's the perfect way for guests to take a break from dancing without feeling removed from the celebration's energy. These seating arrangements also work beautifully during cocktail receptions, offering guests a comfortable space to sip their drinks, catch up with friends, or take in the ambiance of the event.

For after-parties, lounge groupings can help set a more relaxed, intimate vibe. Think plush sofas, chic armchairs, and stylish coffee tables adorned with candles or small floral arrangements.

One of my favorite ways to personalize lounge areas is by adding throw pillows for extra comfort and customizing the covers for a personal touch. Whether it's a monogram, event logo, or a fun design that ties into the celebration's theme, these small details add personality and elegance, making the space feel uniquely yours.

Not only do lounge areas add functionality, but they also enhance the visual flow of your celebration. When thoughtfully placed, they break up large spaces, creating inviting nooks that draw guests in. Lounge groupings are more than just seating—they're an extension of your event's design and a way to ensure guests feel comfortable and cared for throughout the night.

Dancing Shoes for Guests: Keep the Party Going in Comfort

Nothing brings joy and energy to a celebration quite like dancing! Consider offering comfortable dancing shoes for your guests. Whether it's a basket of flip-flops, ballet flats, or slippers, providing a cozy alternative to high heels and dress shoes encourages everyone to hit the dance floor without discomfort. It's a small gesture that speaks volumes about your thoughtfulness and can be customized with monograms or colors that match your event's theme. By prioritizing guest comfort, you ensure the party vibes last well into the night!

Guest Room Blocks

If your celebration includes out-of-town guests, securing room blocks at a nearby hotel is a thoughtful way to ensure their stay is seamless and stress free. Reserving a set of rooms at a discounted rate allows guests to stay close to the venue while enjoying added convenience. Be sure to include the hotel details on your invitations, wedding or event website, or welcome package so guests can easily book their accommodations. This small touch goes a long way in making their travel experience smooth and enjoyable.

As you continue through the other chapters of this book, keep these concepts in mind. Personalization and emotional connection are the threads that tie everything together—from your invitations to your menu, decor, and even the music. Start with the heart of your celebration, and everything else will fall into place.

TIPS FOR DESIGNING EMOTION-DRIVEN CELEBRATIONS

Thoughtful celebrations go beyond beautiful decor—they're designed to stir emotion, spark connection, and stay with your guests long after the last toast. Use these prompts and strategies to guide your planning:

- **Start with emotion:** Define three core feelings you want your guests to experience—joy, nostalgia, warmth—and design around them.
- **Personalize thoughtfully:** Weave in meaningful touches, like a favorite quote on your menu, a family recipe, or decor that tells your story.
- **Welcome with intention:** Set the tone from the start. Greet guests with a signature drink, live music, or a unique design element.
- **Encourage connection:** Create opportunities for interaction—through seating layouts, activities, or thoughtful conversation starters.
- **Surprise and delight:** Plan one unexpected touch, like a curated scent, live artist, or creative food presentation, to leave a lasting impression.

GLOBAL LUXURY
WEDDING PLANNER
AND EVENT DESIGNER,
Akeshi Akinseye
IN COLLABORATION WITH
THE LANGHAM CHICAGO HOTEL
INVITES YOU TO
AN EVENING OF DECADENCE
FEATURING A COCKTAIL RECEPTION,
DINNER EXPERIENCE
AND A FEW SURPRISES
IN CELEBRATION OF THE LAUNCH OF
AKESHI'S NEW DESIGN BOOK
"Festive Tables: A Guide To Setting Stylish Tablescapes For Your Celebrations"
GET READY FOR A NIGHT OF
CURATED EXPERIENCES.
THURSDAY MARCH 9TH, 2023
6:30 PM
The Langham, Chicago
CHICAGO, ILLINOIS
DRESS CODE: GLAM
TREAT YOURSELF A LITTLE LONGER.
THE LANGHAM HOTEL ROOMS ARE
AVAILABLE UPON REQUEST AT A
REDUCED RATE OF
$340 FOR THE NIGHT.
THE LANGHAM HOTEL
330 N WABASH AVE.
CHICAGO, IL 60611
SVP TO AKESHI@KESHEVENTS
BY FEBRUARY 23RD.
PLEASE INCLUDE A
DIETARY RESTRICTIO
WE LOOK FORWARD TO HAVING YOU!
IN EXCHANGE FOR YOUR COMPLIMENTARY
DINING EXPERIENCE WITH US AT
THE LANGHAM, CHICAGO, WE ASK THAT YOU
POST FIVE (5) INSTAGRAM STORIES
SHOWCASING THE EVENT
+ BOOK AND ONE (1) IN-FEED POST.
PLEASE TAG @KESHEVENTS IN
YOUR POSTS. WE SO APPRECIATE
YOU HELPING US SPREAD
THE WORD ABOUT THIS VERY
PASSIONATE PROJECT OF MINE.
WARMLY,
Akeshi

CHAPTER 03

INVITATIONS

Creating the Perfect First Impression.

Now that you've established the foundation and mood of your celebration, it's time to focus on one of the most crucial elements: the invitation. The invitation is the first impression your guests will have of your event, setting the tone and creating a sense of excitement and anticipation. It's not just about informing them of the time and place (though these are crucial elements to include)—it's a reflection of the event's personality, mood, and the experience you want to create. It's important to understand that an invitation is more than just a piece of paper; it's a key part of the overall experience, and it sets the stage for the entire celebration.

I've always believed that the invitation is like a sneak peek into the story your event will tell. Every celebration is an opportunity to craft something unique, and the invitation offers a preview of what's to come. Whether you're planning an intimate gathering, a wedding, or a milestone celebration, the invitation should evoke emotion and curiosity, hinting at the beauty and experiences that await your guests.

For me, this attention to detail started early. Growing up, I watched my mother pour love and care into every event she hosted, and nothing was overlooked, especially the invitation. It wasn't just about formality—it was about setting the stage for what people could expect when they walked through our doors. I've carried this philosophy with me throughout my career.

RSVP
The favor of a reply is re
by Wednesday, July 8
One seat has been reserved in
Please circle your entree choice
Please list any diet
Kindly RSVP for th
jt

Inspiration might come from a wedding's locale—like a chateau in Paris or the South of France—or from personal milestones, such as where the couple got engaged. Whether it's physical or digital, each invitation is crafted to not only inform but to enchant, offering a glimpse of the celebration to come.

As a wedding/event planner, the excitement around crafting invitations is palpable, beginning with the save-the-date. The anticipation builds as these announcements are dispatched to mailboxes or inboxes, eagerly awaiting guests' delighted reactions. Among the many I've cherished, a wine-themed save-the-date remains a standout. Its every detail, from the custom box to the delicately detailed labels and floral accents, was designed to thrill, perfectly echoing the couple's love for wine. This process is always a collaborative effort with stationery designers and clients, turning each invitation into a prelude to the celebration's story.

LAKE STREET
NUMBER 194
CHICAGO, IL
606

THE ART OF CELEBRATING IS ABOUT THOUGHTFUL DECISIONS, AND THE INVITATION IS ONE OF THE FIRST THAT BRINGS YOUR VISION TO LIFE.

ELEMENTS OF A THOUGHTFUL INVITATION

Design Reflects Mood and Theme

The invitation should seamlessly tie into the overall design of your event. Whether you opt for clean, modern lines or soft, romantic details, the invitation must set the tone. Every element, from the paper quality to the color palette and fonts, plays a role in shaping your guests' expectations. Having planned events for over a decade now, I've seen a variety of invitations, each reflecting the mood and personal style of the clients and telling its own story through custom velvet boxes, custom liners, illustrations, foiling, or embossing. Every single detail of the invitations we curate is done with so much care and intention—nothing is random. It's all part of the story the celebration tells from the beginning.

Personalization

Personal touches, like a custom monogram, beautiful calligraphy on the envelope, a custom illustration, or custom stamps can make the invitation feel more intimate and special. It's these little details that will make guests feel like they're part of something meaningful.

Materials and Textures

The tactile experience of an invitation shouldn't be overlooked. Think about how your guests will feel when they touch the paper. I personally love the feel and texture of exquisite paper; the raised, textured foil; the delicate dent of embossing; or the feel of the ribbon. It's all part of the experience. Luxury paper creates an immediate impression of elegance, while natural fibers may signal a more rustic, down-to-earth celebration.

Wording and Tone

The language you choose should reflect the formality (or informality) of your event. The words should be carefully considered to give guests a sense of what to expect. A formal wedding may require traditional phrasing, while a casual dinner party can allow for a more relaxed tone.

Digital Versus Paper Invitations

While paper invitations offer a more personal, tactile experience, digital invitations can still be beautiful and effective when thoughtfully designed. The choice between the two will depend on the event's formality and budget and your personal preference. For grand celebrations, I always recommend paper—it adds a sense of gravitas and thoughtfulness. However, digital can be equally special when designed with care and attention to detail.

“

THOUGHTFUL TIMING ENSURES A STRESS-FREE PLANNING PROCESS FOR BOTH YOU AND YOUR GUESTS.

Timing Matters: Sending Invitations at the Right Moment

The timing of your invitations plays a crucial role in ensuring a smooth guest experience. For weddings, save-the-dates are essential and should be sent six to eight months in advance, allowing guests ample time to make travel arrangements and plan accordingly. These should include key details such as the location, accommodations, and a wedding website (which I highly recommend) for easy access to additional information.

For formal invitations, aim to send them out six to eight weeks before the event—even earlier for destination weddings, where guests may need more time to coordinate logistics. For more casual gatherings, three to four weeks notice is generally sufficient. Regardless of the occasion, always include a clear RSVP deadline, the number of guests allowed, and any key details that will help you manage your guest list efficiently.

The invitation is more than just a formality—it's the starting point for creating a memorable celebration. By putting thought and intention into this first impression, you set the stage for the beauty and joy that will follow.

DESIGNING BEAUTIFUL INVITATIONS

An invitation is the very first touchpoint of the celebration itself. It introduces the theme and style of your event, engaging the senses. As a host, crafting this first impression with intention and care is key. Everything matters: color, font choice, paper selection, design elements, texture, and even scent—all wrapped beautifully in an envelope. For mailed invitations, remember that it's not just paper; it's an experience.

For me, the excitement of planning a celebration often starts with the invitation. And as a host or planner, creating this first impression with intention and attention to detail is key. I can't help but feel the anticipation once they're sent out—it's thrilling to hear guests' reactions as the invitations arrive.

One of the first decisions to make is whether to choose digital or paper invitations. Both have their benefits, but I must admit, there's something magical about a beautifully crafted paper invitation. The texture, the smell, and the surprise of opening it make the experience special, even for more intimate events. The touch of fine paper, the elegance of the design—it all helps set the tone.

That said, digital invitations are practical and can be just as impactful when designed thoughtfully. Even with a digital invite, you want it to feel personal, engaging, and reflective of your event's vibe. It should carry the same wow factor you'd expect from a paper invitation.

SATURDAY, THE SECOND OF SEPTEMBER
TWO-THOUSAND AND TWENTY-THREE
CEREMONY TO COMMENCE AT
BLACK TIE
Kesh Events
730 W Lake Street #8212
Chicago Illinois 60661

Digital Invitations

While digital invitations offer convenience and efficiency, they can still be just as thoughtful and impactful as paper invitations. The key is to ensure that your digital invite reflects the theme and mood of your celebration, while still being personal and engaging. By incorporating design elements that echo your event's vibe and adding special touches, you can create a memorable digital invitation that excites your guests just as much as a physical one.

- **Select a unique design** that reflects the theme and mood of your celebration.
- **Personalize it** with thoughtful wording and your event details.
- **Keep it clean and simple**, ensuring that the invite is easy to read and navigate.
- **Include RSVP management** tools that make it easy for guests to respond and for you to track responses. Be clear on RSVP deadlines, dress codes, and the number of guests allowed.
- **Encourage guests to mention dietary restrictions** when sending their RSVPs.

WELCOME RECEPTION
BLACK TIE RECEPTION
COCKTAIL RECEPTION, DINNER, DANCING,
AND AFTERPARTY
NIZUC RESORT AND SPA
CANCÚN | MEXICO
09/15/2023 - 09/17/2023

Here are some tips to ensure your invitations are just as memorable as the event itself:

- Work with professionals such as a stationery designer and calligrapher for that extra personal touch.
- Choose quality materials. The texture of the paper should reflect the tone of your event, whether that's formal, rustic, or whimsical.
- Don't forget the RSVP card. It's a vital part of managing your guest list. Make it easy for guests to respond and include a return date and any necessary details, like dietary restrictions.
- Add thoughtful details such as pre-stamped envelopes with the return address already printed for the RSVP cards to make it easier for guests to RSVP.
- Consider scent. A subtle fragrance added to the invite can enhance the sensory experience.

The invitation is more than just a formal notice; it's the opening note in the symphony of your celebration. Every design choice, word, and finishing touch should feel intentional, sparking anticipation and excitement.

Paper Invitations

There's something undeniably special about receiving a beautifully crafted paper invitation. The texture, design, and thoughtfulness all work together to set the stage for your upcoming celebration. If you love the feel of a luxurious paper invitation, this is your chance to create a lasting first impression that leaves guests excited for what's to come. Your invitation should reflect the heart and soul of your event, offering guests a tangible sneak peek into the style and mood of the celebration.

TOP SECRET

CREATING AN INVITATION THAT REFLECTS THE CELEBRATION'S THEME AND MOOD

When creating an invitation, it's essential to consider how it will reflect the theme, colors, and tone of the celebration. Whether you're planning a grand wedding, a lunch, an intimate dinner party, or a casual birthday gathering, the invitation should feel like a natural extension of the event itself. Ask yourself:

- What is the overall vibe I want to convey? Elegant? Fun? Relaxed?
- What colors and textures will be present in the event, and how can they be incorporated into the design of the invitation?
- What mood do I want my guests to feel when they receive this invitation—excitement, curiosity, warmth?

THE GUEST EXPERIENCE BEGINS THE MOMENT THEY OPEN THE INVITATION—WHETHER IT'S A BEAUTIFULLY DESIGNED PAPER INVITE OR A THOUGHTFULLY CRAFTED DIGITAL ONE. IT'S YOUR OPPORTUNITY TO MAKE A LASTING FIRST IMPRESSION AND SET THE TONE FOR THE CELEBRATION.

Catering to Guests' Needs

Throughout the process of creating your invitations, from picking the material to finalizing the layout, keep your guests in mind. Think of their experience from the moment they receive the invitation. Will they have all the information they need, like the event website, parking, attire, accommodations? Are there any special considerations they might have? A well-planned invitation takes into account both the joy of the moment and the practical details your guests need to make attending the event seamless.

Managing RSVPs and Guest Lists

Managing RSVPs is crucial to the planning process. For weddings and large events, the RSVP process can become overwhelming, so it's important to have a clear plan in place. Having a structured plan for RSVPs can streamline this often-overwhelming task. First, determine the RSVP deadline, the method of response (mail, email, website), and where responses will be logged.

For easy access and collaboration, consider using a shared, live Google spreadsheet to keep track of RSVPs and special requests. If RSVPs are by mail, ensure that the mailing address is printed clearly, with a dedicated mailbox for responses to avoid any mix-ups. Keep a spreadsheet to track RSVPs and dietary notes, and update it regularly.

Managing Paper Invitations

1. Pre-stamp RSVP envelopes to encourage prompt responses.
2. Add a return address to simplify the process for guests.
3. Include an RSVP deadline (two to three weeks prior for local events, three to four weeks prior for destination events).
4. Follow up politely with guests who haven't responded by the due date.

Managing Digital Invitations

1. Use RSVP tracking tools that come with digital invites to stay organized.
2. Send reminder emails a week before the RSVP deadline for any guests who haven't responded.
3. Make it easy for guests to click and respond with one or two steps.

Response
Kindly reply by
May 14, 2021 online
at
WWW.ARJUNANDALINA.COM
Attire
Formal

Details
N°5
L'EAU
CHANEL
PARIS

Save the Date
AUGUST, 3RD 2019
Kathleen & Jelani
CHICAGO ILLINOIS
formal invitation to follow
KATHLEENANDJELANI.COM

Event Websites

For larger, more complex events such as weddings or destination parties, consider creating an event website. A website can be a helpful tool to share additional information, such as travel details, accommodation recommendations, and itinerary updates. It's an easy way to keep everything in one place and ensure that guests have all the details they need at their fingertips.

RSVP Etiquette

- **Guests RSVPing for more than specified:** Be clear in your RSVP card about the number of guests invited, and politely address any issues where additional guests are added unexpectedly.
- **Following Up on RSVPs:** Whether it's for weddings, birthdays, holidays, or intimate gatherings, following up with guests who haven't responded is important. If you haven't heard back by the RSVP deadline, a gentle reminder via email or text works well. If those attempts don't get a response, a friendly phone call can often do the trick, ensuring your final guest list is in place.
- **Dietary restrictions:** Make sure to ask for any dietary restrictions or preferences in your RSVP card, as this will ensure a smooth experience for your guests when it comes to catering.

GLOBAL LUXURY
WEDDING PLANNER
AND EVENT DESIGNER,
Akeshi Akinseye
IN COLLABORATION WITH
THE LANGHAM CHICAGO HOTEL
INVITES YOU TO
AN EVENING OF DECADENCE
FEATURING A COCKTAIL RECEPTION,
DINNER EXPERIENCE
AND A FEW SURPRISES
IN CELEBRATION OF THE LAUNCH OF
AKESHI'S NEW DESIGN BOOK
"Festive Tables:
A Guide To Setting
Stylish Tablescapes For
Your Celebrations"
GET READY FOR A NIGHT OF
CURATED EXPERIENCES.
THURSDAY MARCH 9TH, 2023
6:30 PM
The Langham, Chicago
CHICAGO, ILLINOIS
DRESS CODE: GLAM

SETTING THE CELEBRATION IN MOTION

The invitation is more than just a formal notice; it's the opening note in the symphony of your celebration. Every design choice, word, and finishing touch should feel intentional, sparking anticipation and excitement. Whether through paper or digital formats, your invitation is the first glimpse guests have of the joy, beauty, and memories that await. As you plan, remember that it's these thoughtful touches that lay the groundwork for a truly unforgettable experience, allowing your guests to feel welcomed, valued, and eagerly awaited.

CRAFTING INVITATIONS THAT SET THE TONE: WHAT TO CONSIDER

- **Match the mood:** Select a design that reflects the event's tone, whether classic, modern, whimsical, or formal. Let the invitation be a visual preview of what's to come.
- **Clarify the details:** Include essential information: date, time, location, dress code, RSVP instructions, and any special notes—without cluttering the layout.
- **Choose your format:** Decide between paper or digital based on your event's formality and your guest list's preferences.
- **Prioritize quality:** For printed invitations, invest in premium papers and finishes that make a lasting first impression.
- **Set RSVP expectations:** Include a clear deadline that allows you ample time to finalize details and confirm headcount.
- **Embrace tech tools:** If going digital, use RSVP tracking features and automated reminders to stay organized and efficient.

CHAPTER 04

MENU PLANNING

A Culinary Experience.

Food is a great way to bring people together. A thoughtfully curated menu does more than nourish the body—it nourishes the soul. It creates moments of joy and connection and memories that last long after the plates are cleared. As an event planner, I've had the privilege of working alongside some of the best chefs, caterers, and culinary experts from around the world.

Whether I'm collaborating on a menu for an intimate dinner party or a grand wedding celebration, the food is always crafted with intention, a reflection of the event's theme, mood, and cultural nuances.

Food has the power to set the tone and create lasting memories for your guests, and that's why it's essential to get it right. The goal is to leave everyone feeling nourished—both in body and spirit.

A Culinary Experience

In this chapter, we'll explore the key elements of creating a memorable culinary experience for your guests, from menu selection and plating to wine pairings and interactive stations. Whether you're hosting a formal dinner, a cocktail party, or a casual gathering, your food and drink offerings should always be a reflection of the celebration itself—beautiful, intentional, and unforgettable.

The menu is not something to be thrown together at the last minute. It's an important part of your event, and like every other aspect of a celebration, it requires intention, thought, and a little creativity. As a host, you need to think beyond just what's on the plate—consider how the entire culinary experience will unfold for your guests. The five senses come into play here. A consummate host always has the five senses in mind, no matter how casual or formal the celebration. From the first bite to the final sip, your menu should delight your guests in taste, smell, sight, touch, and even sound. When crafted with care, the food becomes an integral part of the storytelling, creating conversations, sparking connections, and elevating the entire experience.

CURATING YOUR MENU: FIVE SENSES APPROACH

When I plan menus for my events and for clients, I always consider the five senses. Your dishes should look stunning, smell delightful, taste incredible, and even feel and sound interesting. For example, the crispness of a well-prepared salad or the sizzle of a steak hot off the grill can elevate the dining experience. You want to create dishes that leave a lasting impression, each bite telling a story of the celebration.

The Five Senses:

- **Taste:** Flavor should be balanced and thoughtful. Think of dishes that complement each other rather than competing for attention on the plate.
- **Smell:** The aroma of the food should welcome guests as they arrive, creating an irresistible atmosphere.
- **Sight:** Beautiful plating is essential. Visual appeal sets the stage for the meal before a bite is even taken.
- **Touch:** The textures of the dishes and the place setting should be varied to enhance the experience. Think about how guests will engage with each element of the meal.
- **Sound:** The gentle sizzle of a perfectly seared dish, the satisfying crunch of a crisp bite, or the bubbling of a simmering sauce all contribute to the sensory experience of dining. These subtle yet impactful sounds enhance anticipation and add an extra layer of enjoyment to the meal.

SEASONALITY

When planning your menu, always take the season into account. A summer event might call for fresh salads, grilled seafood, and light, refreshing cocktails, while a fall celebration could feature heartier options like roasted meats, root vegetables, and warm spices.

Summer: Light, fresh, and vibrant dishes that complement the warmer weather. Think refreshing salads, grilled proteins, and fruit-based desserts.
Winter: Comfort foods with bold flavors, warm soups, roasted meats, and decadent desserts.
Spring: Fresh greens, herbs, and light proteins to reflect the season of renewal. Floral notes in both food and drinks can enhance the springtime theme.

LOCATION AND CULTURE

Location plays a major role in curating the menu. Consider what works best in your event's setting—whether it's an intimate indoor gathering or an outdoor garden party.

Culture is another important factor. As a Nigerian, I love incorporating a bit of my heritage into my events. Food is a way to show love and connect with people. The flavors, tastes, and aromas of my Nigerian upbringing often inspire my menus, whether it's through a flavorful dish, a unique dessert, or even a creative cocktail. Don't be afraid to infuse elements of your culture or personal experiences into the menu—it makes the culinary experience even more special.

FOOD

Food is often the highlight of any celebration, making it essential to craft a menu that complements your theme and leaves a lasting impression on your guests. When planning the menu, consider the season, dietary restrictions, and the formality of the event. The food and drink menu is a key component of any celebration, and believe me, it's what guests look forward to the most. The decor, entertainment, and ambiance are essential, but the menu tops the list. Therefore, your menu should be thoughtfully curated to match the theme, season, location, and even culture of the event.

Dietary Restrictions

Addressing dietary restrictions is crucial when planning your event's menu to ensure all guests enjoy their meal safely. Including an option for guests to communicate any dietary needs on the invitation is essential. This proactive approach helps avoid potential issues, such as guests having allergic reactions. Work closely with your catering team to craft alternatives that are as delicious and enticing as the main offerings.

Being a thoughtful host means ensuring that all guests feel included and cared for. Provide a variety of options like vegetarian, gluten-free, and allergen-friendly dishes. Ask for dietary preferences on your RSVP cards and collaborate with your caterer to ensure these alternatives align with the event's theme and flavor profile. This attention to detail ensures that every guest can fully enjoy the celebration, regardless of dietary restrictions.

Party Starters

Every celebration starts with a first impression, and your menu should be no different. Guests often arrive hungry and excited, so begin the experience with party starters, whether passed hors d'oeuvres or stationed on beautifully styled platters. This sets the tone for what's to come and gives your guests a little taste of what's ahead.

When planning your starters, think of dishes that are easy to eat yet packed with flavor or even elements of surprise like the pairings, styling, or displays. Personally, I like a drink upon arrival versus food in your faceYou want guests to ease into the space and experience.

For passed hors d'oeuvres, consider bite-sized pieces that guests can easily enjoy while mingling. For food stations, think of how the presentation can enhance the theme. Even small bites can make a big impact if presented thoughtfully. Remember that timing is everything. Plan your event out, and time the food-serving.

Food Stations and Displays

For more casual events or cocktail parties, consider using food stations. They allow guests to graze and try different options at their own pace. The same goes for weddings, at the cocktail reception. Think of fun stations like a seafood station adorned with decor or an ice sculpture with your monogram. There are a ton of ideas, so don't be afraid to get creative and explore different kinds of food displays. The presentation of these stations should be just as thoughtful as the food itself. Use trays, platters, and stands that enhance the theme and elevate the guest experience.

Dress up your food stations with pops of florals, decor, or a grand centerpiece, depending on the layout. Safely placed candles can make a world of difference in creating ambiance. I also love to include menu signs for each station, adding a thoughtful and polished touch to the presentation.

Styling Food Stations

When styling food stations, think of them as mini stages for your culinary display. Using tiered platters and stands adds height and visual interest, making the station feel abundant. Incorporate fresh florals and design elements that tie into your event's theme, and consider a beautiful linen to dress the table. Plan for easy guest flow—ensure guests can access food and serving utensils easily. If your event has a large guest count, consider multiple stations to avoid congestion.

Food Tags

When serving food at stations or passing appetizers, don't underestimate the value of well-designed food tags. Clearly labeling each dish not only informs guests about what they're enjoying but also highlights key dietary considerations, saving them from having to ask, "What's this?" Food tags can also be placed on trays for passed hors d'oeuvres, ensuring a seamless and enjoyable dining experience where guests can confidently make their selections.

More Food Considerations

- **Food temperature:** Use chafing dishes or other warming solutions to keep food hot.
- **Station stability:** Choose a sturdy table to support heavier platters.
- **Strategic placement:** Set up stations near seating or social areas to keep guests mingling close by.

DESSERTS

Think beyond traditional dessert presentations and turn them into an unforgettable experience. Instead of serving a standard plated dessert, consider interactive and visually captivating options. For example, we've elevated dessert service by rolling out beautifully styled carts filled with an assortment of sweet treats, allowing guests to choose their favorites tableside, adding an element of surprise and delight. In other instances, I've curated individually designed mini cakes for each guest, customized to reflect the colors and style of the celebration. Thoughtful touches like these transform dessert into more than just the final course; they become a highlight of the event, leaving a lasting impression.

To elevate the dessert experience further, consider incorporating a sophisticated touch with beverages. For example, at some events, we've introduced passed mini espresso martinis alongside the dessert carts, blending the rich flavors of coffee and vodka for a delightful cap to the meal.

At one particular celebration, we even designed a custom espresso martini bar to complement the dessert offerings, adding an elegant and interactive element to the evening that guests thoroughly enjoyed. This combination of unique desserts and bespoke beverages ensures a memorable ending to any event.

THE BOUIE WEDDING

LATE-NIGHT BITES: THE PERFECT FINISH TO KEEP GUESTS ENGAGED

Late-night bites are a fantastic way to keep energy high and give guests something memorable to savor as the celebration unfolds. Many guests may feel overwhelmed during the main course or not fully satisfy their appetite, so providing delicious late-night snacks can be a welcome treat. Think of fun, satisfying bites like sliders, pizza slices, or truffle fries.

Add a touch of creativity with personalized food boxes, labels, or picks featuring your event theme, monogram, or a special message. These thoughtfully crafted mini bites serve to keep guests happy, energized, and entertained well into the evening, adding a surprise that they'll fondly remember.

DRINKS, COCKTAILS, AND WINE

People often focus heavily on food and put little thought into the drink experience, but the drink menu is just as important. Your beverage offerings should be fun, engaging, and inclusive, catering to both those who enjoy alcohol and those who don't. Consider signature cocktails that align with your event's theme, but also ensure your nonalcoholic options are equally special. Too often, nondrinkers are offered nothing more than juice or water, but I highly disagree with this approach. Guests who choose not to drink deserve the same level of thought and attention. For example, if you're serving champagne, offer a nonalcoholic sparkling alternative. Your guests will truly appreciate the extra consideration.

THE ELEGANT TOUCHES YOU ADD TO YOUR BAR OR BAR CART WILL NOT GO UNNOTICED—THESE SMALL BUT IMPACTFUL DETAILS ELEVATE THE DRINK EXPERIENCE AND ENHANCE THE OVERALL CELEBRATION.

The way drinks are served is key to the overall experience. Personally, I believe the drink experience begins with the making or display of the beverage. The glassware, the garnish, the presentation—these elements enhance the experience and make it feel more thoughtful and curated. For larger events, having a professional bartender or a mixologist can elevate the experience by ensuring drinks are served smoothly and correctly, freeing you to focus on your guests and enjoy the party.

Styling Your Bar and Drinks

The elegant touches you add to your bar or bar cart will not go unnoticed, so put some thought into how you want to style these areas. Consider using seasonal colors and flavors for garnishes to tie everything together. I personally love incorporating personalized elements, like custom cocktail napkins and stirrers, which can easily be designed and ordered online. These small but impactful details will elevate your drink presentation and enhance the overall guest experience.

Wine Pairings and Bar Setup

- **Wine pairings:** Offer a variety of red, white, and sparkling wines to pair with your courses. A professional bartender, caterer, or sommelier can assist in selecting the perfect wines for your menu, ensuring everything flows seamlessly.
- **Bar setup:** Don't overlook the importance of the bar setup. Ensure you have the proper glassware—champagne flutes, wine glasses for red and white wine, beautiful cocktail glasses, and water goblets. Keep extras on hand, and consider the length of your event to calculate how much you'll need.
- **Accessories:** In addition to beautifully curated drinks and glassware, I love adding elegant cocktail napkins, cocktail stirrers, and personalized bar signage. Years ago, my friend By Dami Studios created a crest and monogram for me, which we've used to design so many fun bar accessories at my events—from bar signage to cocktail napkins, dinner napkins, stirrers, and more. These details add a level of personalization and elevate the entire experience. My motto on my monogram is *"Live, Love, Party"* and it perfectly captures the spirit I aim to bring to every celebration.

The Bowie
ESPRESSO MARTINI BAR
Indulge in a signature
Espresso Martini
a perfect blend of:
Vodka, Fresh Espresso, Coffee Liqueur
and Demerara Syrup
Cheers to love, laughter, and luxury!

Sip and Repeat
BECAUSE NO GREAT DINNER
PARTY EVER STARTED
WITH SOMEONE EATING A SALAD
Grab a Drink
HERE ARE AKESHI'S FAVORITES
FRENCH MARTINI WITH A TWIST
VODKA, PINEAPPLE, RASPBERRY
OLD FASHIONED WITH A TWIST
BOURBON, SCHLITZ DEMERARA, BITTERS

LIVE • LOVE • PARTY
MORE COCKTAILS PLEASE!

Menu
STARTER
Atlantic scallops with ribbons
of vegetables and a fresh herb salad
Trou Normand
Citrus sorbet with Lemon & Vodka
ENTRÉE
Fillet of sea bream with
extra virgin olive oil with vegetables
Tourneдos of fillet steak 'Rossini'
& creamy parmesan polenta
SIDES
Moi Moi
Jollof Rice
Plantain
Dessert
Lemon Velvet Cake

THE MENU CARD

Encompassing your event's food and drink offerings, the often-underrated menu card can be an experience in itself. It's not just about listing what's being served—it's a way to add another layer of style and detail to your event, adding a personal touch to the celebration.

Personally, I find great joy in designing menu cards. For me, it's like giving a gift to my guests, because every detail is designed with love and intention. From the shape and texture to the colors and fonts, each element is thoughtfully curated to reflect the event's theme and tone. It's thrilling to see guests take their seats, and one of the first things they gravitate toward is the menu card. Watching their faces light up as they read it, knowing how much care went into creating it, is one of my favorite parts of hosting.

Having planned hundreds of events, I've learned that a well-designed menu card is more than just practical—it elevates the entire dining experience, offering guests a preview of the culinary journey that awaits them. Whether it's a formal dinner or a casual gathering, I believe the menu card can enhance the anticipation and excitement of the meal.

A well-designed menu card can tie in with your event's overall aesthetic and give guests a preview of the delicious journey they're about to embark on.

For a formal event, a detailed menu card with descriptions of each dish and wine pairing is ideal. Don't forget to include important details like dietary considerations and allergen information. For more casual events, such as a picnic or lunch, a simpler, more playful menu card can be used. These can easily be designed using templates available online and printed from home.

Just be sure to plan ahead. Don't wait until the last minute to print your menu cards.

“

ONE OF THE MOST IMPORTANT PIECES OF ADVICE I CAN OFFER IS TO KNOW YOUR LIMITS AS A HOST.

HIRING HELP: CATERERS AND BARTENDERS

As a host, you can't do everything yourself. Hiring a professional caterer and bartender ensures that everything runs smoothly, from food prep to service. A professional team will help you curate the perfect menu and allow you to enjoy your celebration alongside your guests without worrying about the logistics.

- **Caterers:** A good caterer will work with you to design a menu that aligns with your theme, dietary restrictions, and culinary preferences. They know the trends in the culinary space and have the creative ability to elevate the food and drink experience, and free you as a host to enjoy your celebration.
- **Servers:** If you choose to cook yourself but have limited help with keeping the food warm and presentable, serving guests, and cleaning up throughout the event, consider hiring professional servers so you are not stretched thin, frazzled, and overwhelmed during your event.
- **Bartenders:** Having a professional bartender means that your guests' drinks will always be on point, and you won't have to worry about running out of supplies or keeping up with drink requests.
- **Mixologists:** As a global planner working with discerning guests, working with a mixologist is a delightful addition, elevating the beverage experience by creating custom, sophisticated cocktails that complement the overall event atmosphere. This expertise not only impresses guests but also adds a layer of refinement and entertainment to your celebration.

For Event-Planning Success

- **Research and vet your vendors:** Don't try to do it all yourself. Take time to research and thoroughly vet your caterer, chef, or food provider. Look at reviews, request tastings, and ask questions to ensure they align with your vision and standards. The right professional will help execute your menu flawlessly and elevate your guest experience.
- **Use seasonal and local ingredients:** Whenever possible, choose ingredients that are in season and locally sourced. Not only do they taste better, but they also support local farmers and purveyors.
- **Create interactive stations:** For larger events, consider incorporating food stations where guests can interact with the chef or customize their meal. This adds an engaging and personal touch to the dining experience.

When it comes to creating an unforgettable event, the culinary experience is a critical part of the equation. Plan with intention, thinking through every detail—from the food and drink to the presentation and service. Curate a menu that not only reflects the season and location but also incorporates personal touches that will resonate with your guests. A well-executed culinary experience will ensure your event is remembered fondly by all who attend.

With the right foundation, you can bring your dreams to life and create an unforgettable experience for your guests. Remember that every great celebration starts with careful planning and a clear vision, and the way to your guests' hearts is often through their stomachs.

DESIGNING A MEANINGFUL MENU: TIPS TO GUIDE YOUR PLANNING

- **Engage the five senses:** Plan a menu that delights with flavor, aroma, texture, and presentation. Even the sound of a sizzling dish or clinking glasses adds to the atmosphere.
- **Celebrate the season:** Incorporate seasonal ingredients for vibrant, fresh flavors that align with the time of year and feel intentional.
- **Infuse personal meaning:** Draw inspiration from your heritage, favorite dishes, or travels to make your menu feel uniquely yours.
- **Accommodate with care:** Offer options that consider dietary needs (vegetarian, gluten-free, allergen-conscious), ensuring all guests feel welcomed.
- **Elevate with drinks:** Don't overlook beverages—signature cocktails and thoughtfully crafted nonalcoholic options round out the experience.
- **Bring in professionals:** Skilled caterers and bartenders ensure smooth service, freeing you to focus on celebrating with your guests.

CHAPTER 05

COOKING

Party Favorites from My Nigerian Childhood.

Cooking is an essential element of every celebration, no matter the scale. A well-curated menu brings people together, nourishing not just their bodies but also their spirits. It's more than a necessity—it's an act of love, a way to tell stories, and a beautiful bridge between generations. For me, cooking is also deeply personal. It's a connection to my roots, my family, and the cherished memories of my childhood in Nigeria.

This chapter is my way of paying homage to my mom and the unforgettable dishes she made for every gathering. Our family celebrations were never complete without the mouthwatering aromas of her cooking filling the air and drawing everyone to the table. Her meals brought people together, not just to eat, but to connect, laugh, and share moments of pure joy.

Party Favorites from My Nigerian Childhood

The recipes I'm sharing in this chapter are a taste of those experiences—simple, flavorful dishes that were staples at our family parties. Jollof Rice, meat pies, and Puff Puff are just a few of the dishes that filled my childhood with warmth and flavor. Passed down from my mother and perfected in my own kitchen, they reflect the love, pride, and creativity she poured into every meal. They are now my way of sharing a piece of my heritage with you.

I invite you to try these dishes and bring a little piece of my childhood to your table. Feel free to make them your own—add your favorite spices, tweak the flavors, or serve them with your unique twist. Cooking, after all, is about sharing, experimenting, and creating memories. These recipes are an open invitation to celebrate, connect, and carry on traditions filled with love and warmth.

Before You Begin: Hosting & Cooking Considerations

As you prepare to bring these flavors to life in your own kitchen, here are a few thoughtful considerations to guide your experience—from planning your menu to plating with intention:

- **Think in batches:** Many dishes are designed for gatherings, so consider doubling your recipes to feed a crowd or save time during prep.
- **Stay flexible:** If certain spices or ingredients aren't readily available, don't hesitate to adapt. Focus on capturing the essence, not perfection.
- **Plan your pairings:** As you build your menu, think about variety in texture, temperature, and flavor to create a balanced experience.
- **Style your presentation:** Beautiful plating goes a long way. Elevate your serving with fresh garnishes, simple styling, or coordinated tableware.
- **Embrace the journey:** Whether you're familiar or just discovering these cultural flavors, let the process be joyful and explorative.
- **Share the meaning:** A story behind the dish adds richness. When serving guests, offer a few words about the tradition or inspiration behind what's on the table.

FEATURED *RECIPES*

Nigerian Meat Pies

Nigerian meat pies, with their flaky crust and savory filling, are a beloved party snack. Whether enjoyed on their own or paired with a dipping sauce, they're a celebration essential that combines tradition and versatility.

Growing up, no party menu felt complete without Nigerian meat pies—savory pockets of joy that filled every gathering with irresistible aroma and flavor. Known for their flaky crust and deliciously seasoned beef filling, these patties were always a crowd-pleaser. I love how versatile the ingredients can be—you can swap the beef for chicken or turkey or add vegetables like carrots and potatoes to your taste. When I moved to Chicago, I called my mom for the recipe to ease my homesickness, and over the years, I've added my own touches.

These treats make the perfect addition to any party, offering a savory, cozy bite with veggies and rich flavors. Both elegant and hearty, they're a deliciously nostalgic choice for any gathering. Feel free to experiment with the recipe by using chicken, turkey, or even adding extra vegetables, or keep it strictly vegetables.

INGREDIENTS

- 3 cups all-purpose flour
- 1/2 tsp salt
- 3/4 tsp baking powder
- 1/4 nutmeg
- 3/4 cup salted butter (12 tbsp), chilled and cubed
- 1/2 cup milk
- 1 tbsp vegetable oil
- 1 small onion, chopped
- 2 cloves garlic, minced
- 1 lb ground beef
- 1 medium potato, peeled and diced
- 1 medium carrot, peeled and diced
- 1 tbsp curry powder
- 1 tsp dried thyme
- 1/2 tsp salt
- 1/4 tsp black pepper
- Seasoning powder (e.g., Knorr)
- 1 egg, beaten (for egg wash)

DIRECTIONS

1. **Prepare the dough:** In a large mixing bowl, combine flour, salt, nutmeg and baking powder. Add chilled butter cubes and mix until it resembles coarse crumbs. Gradually add cold milk and mix until the dough forms. Knead on a floured surface for a few minutes until smooth.
2. **Prepare the filling:** Preheat oven to 375°F. In a skillet, heat vegetable oil over medium-high heat. Sauté onion and garlic for 2–3 minutes. Add ground beef, cooking until browned (5–7 minutes). Add potato, carrot, curry powder, thyme, salt, pepper, and seasoning cube, stirring well. Cook for 5–7 minutes until vegetables are tender, then let it cool.
3. **Assemble the patties:** Roll out the dough on a floured surface to about 1/8-inch thickness. Use a 6" empanada press maker or dumpling maker. Place the dough in the empanada maker and place a spoonful of the beef filling in the center of each dough circle and fold.
4. **Bake:** Whisk 1 egg and brush each patty with beaten egg. Place patties on a baking sheet pan and bake for 20–25 minutes, until golden brown.
5. **Serve:** Enjoy warm or at room temperature. Perfect as a snack or for special celebrations.

Sausage Rolls

These flaky pastries, filled with seasoned sausage, were the highlight of my school lunch boxes and family parties alike. Their warm, comforting flavor still takes me back to my childhood kitchen, where I'd watch my mother create these delightful treats.

Growing up, cooking and baking were daily routines in our home, and some of my favorite memories were the delicious snacks my mother would make for school lunches. She'd fill our lunch boxes with treats, like sausage rolls that smelled so amazing I could hardly wait to eat them. In Nigeria, sausage rolls are a popular snack, made from a flaky pastry wrapped around a well-seasoned sausage filling. This simple recipe brings back those cherished childhood memories and is perfect for any occasion.

INGREDIENTS

- 2 cups all-purpose flour
- ¾ tsp baking powder
- 2 eggs (one for dough, one yolk for brushing)
- ½ tbsp salt
- ¾ cup salted butter, chilled and cubed
- ½ cup cold milk
- Sausage pieces

DIRECTIONS

1. **Prepare the dough:** In a large mixing bowl, combine the flour, egg, pinch of salt, and butter. Mix until it resembles coarse crumbs.
2. **Knead and rest:** Gradually add cold milk, and knead the dough until smooth. Cover and let it rest for about 1 hour.
3. **Cook the sausage:** Gently cook the sausage (optional to add spices). Avoid browning.
4. **Preheat and roll out dough:** Preheat oven to 375°F. Roll out the dough on a floured surface to about ⅛-inch thickness.
5. **Shape rolls:** Cut the dough into 3-inch strips, place a sausage piece at one end, and roll until fully wrapped. Trim off any excess dough.
6. **Repeat:** Repeat with remaining dough and sausage pieces.
7. **Brush and bake:** Brush each sausage roll with egg yolk. Arrange on a baking sheet, leaving space between each. Bake for about 15–20 minutes, or until lightly golden.

Serve these savory rolls warm, as an appetizer or snack at any gathering!

Jollof Rice

Known as the ultimate West African party dish, Jollof Rice is vibrant, smoky, and packed with flavor. This one-pot wonder is a staple at Nigerian celebrations, and a dish I can't imagine a gathering without.

In Nigerian cuisine, Jollof Rice is traditionally made with ingredients like tomato puree, Scotch bonnet peppers, onions, and a blend of spices that includes thyme, curry powder, and bay leaves, all simmered in a savory broth. The magic of Jollof lies in its ability to pair seamlessly with an array of proteins—from chicken and turkey to beef, lamb, and fish—making it both a hearty main course and a perfect accompaniment. While recipes and preparation methods vary across countries, each region's unique take on Jollof adds to its charm and versatility.

I can't think of a more iconic West African dish than Jollof Rice. Back home and even here in the United States, no Nigerian celebration feels complete without it. Its vibrant color and rich, smoky flavor are a testament to the joy of gathering and the warmth and hospitality that come with sharing a meal. For me, Jollof Rice is a cherished tradition, a shared experience, and a delicious reminder of home.

INGREDIENTS

For the rice and sauce base:

- 2–3 red bell peppers
- 4-5 large tomatoes, roughly chopped
- 1 medium onion, chopped, divided
- 1 Scotch bonnet pepper
- 3 cloves garlic, minced
- 1 tbsp fresh ginger, minced or grated
- 6 tbsp oil
- 2 tbsp tomato paste
- 2 tsp curry powder
- 1 tsp thyme
- Salt to taste
- 2 stock cubes (bouillon cubes)
- 3 cups long-grain rice
- 2 cups chicken stock (or beef/vegetable stock)
- 2 bay leaves

DIRECTIONS

1. **Preheat the oven:** Preheat your oven to 350°F while you prepare the ingredients.
2. **Prepare the sauce:** In a blender, combine the red bell peppers, tomatoes, half of the chopped onion, Scotch bonnet, garlic, and ginger. Blend until smooth, then set aside.
3. **Build the flavor base:** Heat oil in an oven-safe pot or pan over medium heat. Add the remaining chopped onion and sauté for 3–5 minutes until they're soft and translucent. Add the tomato paste to the onions and fry for about 5 minutes, stirring occasionally. This step deepens the tomato flavor and gives the rice its rich color.
4. **Add spices and seasonings:** Stir in the curry powder, thyme, salt, and stock cubes. Continue to cook for a couple of minutes, then add the blended tomato mixture. Let this sauce cook, stirring occasionally, for 10–15 minutes until it thickens and the oil starts to separate from the sauce.
5. **Combine the rice and sauce:** Add the rice to the pot, stirring until each grain is well-coated with the sauce. Pour in the chicken stock and add the bay leaves. Stir briefly, cover the pot tightly with a lid (or foil, if the lid isn't tight fitting), and bring it to a rolling boil on the stovetop.
6. **Bake in the oven:** Place the pot in the preheated oven and bake for 45 minutes to 1 hour. Check halfway through, stir the rice, and adjust seasoning if needed. If you prefer softer rice, add an extra ½ cup of water and continue baking for another 15–20 minutes.
7. **Serve:** Once cooked, remove the pot from the oven, fluff the rice with a fork, and taste for seasoning. Serve hot, garnished with fresh herbs, alongside coleslaw, salad, or your choice of protein.

Puff Puff

Light, airy, and slightly sweet, Puff Puff is the perfect snack or dessert. These golden, fried dough balls were always the first to disappear from party platters during my childhood celebrations.

Puff Puff is a tasty West African snack, particularly popular in Nigeria. It consists of fried dough balls that are slightly sweet and crispy on the outside, yet soft and fluffy inside. While the name "Puff Puff" is commonly used in Nigeria, many countries across Africa have their own names and versions of this delightful treat. Though simple in ingredients, Puff Puff is a staple at gatherings and celebrations, offering a taste of tradition and nostalgia with every bite. These golden, pillowy, fried dough balls are slightly sweet and wonderfully addictive.

Puff Puff holds a special place in my heart, reminding me of the lively celebrations of my childhood. Growing up, no party was complete without these delicious bites, and I remember eagerly waiting for the first batch to come out of the hot oil. Whether served plain or dusted with powdered sugar, Puff Puff always brings back those nostalgic memories of family, joy, and celebration.

To elevate Puff Puff as a dessert, slice through one or two pieces and plate with a scoop of ice cream. For an extra treat, add fresh fruit garnishes and drizzle with chocolate sauce. Dusting with powdered sugar over the plate creates a beautiful, indulgent dessert experience.

Puff Puff is perfect for casual gatherings, dessert stations, or as a fun snack during cocktail hour.
Enjoyed on its own as a warm, lightly dusted appetizer, this treat brings a touch of sweetness that's sure to delight. It's simple yet unforgettable—much like the cherished celebrations of my childhood.

INGREDIENTS

- 2 cups all-purpose flour
- 2 cups water
- 1/2 cup sugar
- 2 tsp yeast
- 1/2 tsp salt
- 1 tsp vanilla extract (optional)
- 1/4 tsp ground nutmeg (optional)
- Vegetable oil, for frying
- *Optional*: Powdered sugar for dusting

DIRECTIONS

1. **Prepare the batter:** In a large bowl, combine flour, sugar, yeast, salt, vanilla extract and nutmeg (if using). Gradually add warm water while mixing to form a thick, smooth batter. Cover the bowl with a cloth and allow the dough to rise for about 2–2.5 hours, or until doubled in size.
2. **Heat the oil:** Add oil to a pot to reach about 2 inches deep. Heat oil in a deep pan over medium heat. The oil should be deep enough to submerge the Puff Puff balls completely. Heat on medium until a drop of batter rises to the surface.
3. **Fry the Puff Puff:** Once the oil is hot, scoop small portions of the dough (using your hands or a small spoon) and carefully drop them into the oil. Fry until golden brown on all sides, turning occasionally to ensure even cooking. This should take about 3–5 minutes per batch.
4. **Drain and serve:** Once fried, remove the Puff Puff from the oil and drain on paper towels. Dust with powdered sugar if desired and serve warm.

Peppered Snails

A luxurious Nigerian delicacy, peppered snail is loved for its tender, slightly chewy texture paired with a bold, spicy kick. This dish is a must-try for adventurous food lovers and a standout addition to any celebration, symbolizing the vibrancy of Nigerian flavors. Whether served as an appetizer or part of a main course, peppered snail is sure to impress.

INGREDIENTS

- 8–10 fresh snails (cleaned thoroughly)
- 2 tbsp lime or lemon juice (for cleaning)
- 2 medium onions, chopped, divided
- 1 tsp ginger powder
- 1 tsp garlic powder
- 1 tsp thyme
- 1 tsp curry powder
- Salt to taste
- 4 fresh toatoes, chopped
- 2–3 Scotch bonnet peppers (adjust to spice preference)
- 2 tbsp vegetable oil
- 1 bouillon cube
- 1 red and 1 green bell pepper for serving

DIRECTIONS

1. **Prepare the snails:** Thoroughly clean the snails with lime or lemon juice and water to remove slime. Rinse repeatedly until clean.
2. **Boil the snails:** In a pot, combine snails, half the onions, ginger powder, garlic powder, thyme, curry powder, and a pinch of salt. Add water to cover and boil for 20–30 minutes until tender. Drain and set aside.
3. **Prepare the pepper sauce:** Blend tomatoes, Scotch bonnet peppers, and remaining onions into a coarse mixture. Heat vegetable oil in a pan, add the blended mix, and cook for 10–12 minutes until the oil separates from the sauce.
4. **Combine snails and sauce:** Add the boiled snails to the sauce, stir well, and season with a bouillon cube and salt. Cook for another 5 minutes, allowing the snails to absorb the flavors.
5. **Serve:** Garnish with sliced fresh peppers or onions, and serve as an appetizer or alongside Jollof Rice for a complete meal.

Enjoy the bold, spicy, and tender flavors of this iconic Nigerian dish!

Beef Suya

Beef Suya is considered Nigerian street food, with tender, spiced, and smoky beef skewers. Traditionally found in Nigerian cities at night, Suya is crafted by skilled vendors known as Malams. For me, Suya is pure nostalgia. Every visit home, I crave this savory delight, with its smoky aroma, heat, and zest.

In Nigeria, Suya skewers are served with sliced tomatoes and onions. The secret lies in the Suya spice (Yaji)—a bold blend of ground peanuts, chili, ginger, garlic, and onion powders. This distinctive nutty seasoning brings out a savory, slightly sweet, and spicy flavor that elevates meats, especially in traditional Nigerian street foods like Suya skewers, by adding layers of complexity and intensity to each bite. Although traditionally grilled over open flames, Suya can also be made in the oven or stove, yielding delicious results without the char of an open flame. With its unique flavors and a kick of spice, Suya is unlike any other grilled meat. Let's dive into this recipe, so you can bring a taste of Nigeria to your table.

INGREDIENTS

- 1 lb thinly sliced beef (top sirloin or flank steak)
- 2–3 tbsp Suya spice (Yaji), or more to taste (available in African markets and stores)
- 1/2 tsp salt
- 1–2 tbsp vegetable oil
- ***Optional***: Additional seasoning, such as bouillon or cayenne pepper
- Bamboo skewers (soaked in water for 30 minutes)
- Sliced onions and tomatoes (for garnish)

DIRECTIONS

1. **Prepare the beef:** Place the sliced beef in a large bowl. Add salt and Suya spice, tossing until evenly coated.
2. **Marinate:** Drizzle oil over the seasoned beef and mix. Let marinate for at least 30 minutes (up to 2 hours for a richer flavor).
3. **Skewer the beef:** Thread beef strips onto soaked skewers, spacing for even cooking.
4. **Grill or bake:** Preheat grill to medium-high heat. Grill for 5–7 minutes per side, until edges are charred. If baking, preheat oven to 425°F, and bake for 10–12 minutes, turning halfway.
5. **Serve:** Arrange skewers with sliced onions and tomatoes.

TIPS FOR PERFECT SUYA

- For extra tenderness, let the meat marinate as long as possible. A minimum of 4 hours is recommended, but overnight is ideal.
- When grilling, be cautious not to overcook the beef, as it's sliced thinly and cooks quickly.
- For added flavor, sprinkle the Suya spice blend on the meat as soon as it's off the grill, giving it an extra boost of flavor

COOKING IS AN ART THAT BRINGS PEOPLE TOGETHER, ONE PLATE AT A TIME.

Each recipe in this chapter, from childhood dishes to cultural classics, is a testament to the joy and warmth that food can bring to a celebration. When we cook, we're not only nourishing our bodies but also crafting memories, sharing stories, and celebrating life's moments. As you prepare these dishes, remember that every stir, every taste, and every sprinkle of spice is an opportunity to connect with those you love. So, dive into these recipes with an open heart, and let your kitchen become a place where traditions are celebrated, and new memories are made.

Cooking Considerations: Creating a Meaningful Culinary Experience

Before you step into the kitchen, take a moment to reflect on how your menu can enhance the celebration and tell a deeper story. These considerations are here to guide you as you plan and prepare with purpose:

- **Choose recipes with meaning:** Opt for dishes that reflect your cultural heritage, seasonal ingredients, or personal favorites to create a heartfelt connection.
- **Balance flavor and ease:** A variety of textures and flavors is key, but so is managing your time. Select recipes that are both delicious and realistic for your scale.
- **Test ahead:** If a recipe is new or hasn't been made in a while, give it a trial run. A quick test brings confidence—and a better guest experience.
- **Plan and prep:** Chop, marinate, or bake in advance when possible. A little prep goes a long way on the day of your event.
- **Make it joyful:** Put on music, invite someone to cook with you, or simply allow yourself to be fully present. The process should be as fulfilling as the meal itself.

brunch

CHAPTER 06

SIGNATURE DRINKS

Toasting to the Occasion.

In every celebration, drinks hold a special place—they're more than just beverages; they're a part of the experience, a toast to moments that bring us together. From the first sip to the last, a thoughtfully crafted drink can elevate the mood, engage the senses, and leave a lasting impression. Whether it's a lively cocktail or a refreshing mocktail, signature drinks can set the tone, echo the event's theme, and add a touch of elegance that guests will remember.

When I think of celebrations, I envision the sound of glasses clinking, the colorful garnishes catching the eye, and the flavors that capture the essence of the moment. In this chapter, we'll explore how to create signature drinks that add flair, warmth, and a personal touch to your event. From choosing the right ingredients to perfecting the presentation, these drinks will bring your celebration to life, one glass at a time.

Toasting Occasion

I especially love curating the drink experience with the caterers, venues, and mixologists we collaborate with because it's so much fun to see the possibilities and how something that might be considered simple can become a whole experience on its own. For a couple's post-wedding brunch celebration, we styled a welcome cart with colorful, and might I add delicious, welcome cocktails with umbrellas, signage, and straws that said "brunch" and a customized version for the happy couple that said "bride and groom." Furthermore, the bar featured exciting cocktails, mocktails, and a full-service bar for this incredible brunch celebration. Guests were greeted right off the elevator with welcome drinks, music, decor and amazing company.

Additionally, balancing flavors is essential. A great cocktail should have a harmony of sweet, sour, bitter, and sometimes even spicy notes. Try incorporating unique ingredients like basil, rosemary, or infused syrups to elevate traditional flavors. By thoughtfully selecting every element—from spirits to garnishes—you can create a cocktail experience that is as memorable and enjoyable as the celebration itself.

Welcome Drinks

As I've shared in previous chapters, first impressions matter, especially at celebrations, where your welcome drink sets the tone for the entire event. Tailor these drinks to the occasion, season, and sometimes even your personal preference to create a delightful and welcoming experience.

Crafting the drink experience is like creating a work of art—it's a blend of flavors, colors, and textures that should harmonize with the event's mood and theme. When selecting ingredients, consider the colors and garnishes that will enhance the visual appeal, such as fresh herbs, citrus slices, decorative ice cubes or edible flowers that add elegance and a pop of color.

Seasonal Welcome Drinks

- **Spring: Sparkling Elderflower Lemonade**

A refreshing, floral lemonade with a hint of sparkle
Recipe: Combine fresh lemon juice, elderflower syrup, sparkling water, and a touch of simple syrup.
Garnish: Edible flowers like pansies or a lemon wheel

- **Spring: Lavender Lemon Spritz (Zero-Proof)**

A light and fragrant spritz infused with lavender syrup
Recipe: Mix lavender syrup, fresh lemon juice, and sparkling water over ice.
Garnish: Fresh lavender sprig or a lemon twist

- **Summer: Rosé Sangria**

A fruity, chilled cocktail that's perfect for warm-weather gatherings
Recipe: Combine rosé wine, sliced peaches, strawberries, and a splash of orange liqueur. Chill and serve over ice.
Garnish: Fresh mint and a strawberry slice

- **Summer: Tropical Mango Mocktail (Zero-Proof)**

A tropical, sweet treat bursting with mango flavor
Recipe: Blend fresh mango juice, lime juice, and soda water. Add a splash of coconut water for an island-inspired twist.
Garnish: Lime wheel or a slice of mango on the rim

- **Autumn: Apple Cider Mimosa**

A crisp and bubbly fall favorite with a touch of warmth
Recipe: Mix chilled apple cider with sparkling wine or champagne.
Garnish: Cinnamon stick or a thin apple slice

- **Autumn: Cranberry-Ginger Sparkler (Zero-Proof)**

A tangy, ginger-infused drink that's both festive and refreshing
Recipe: Combine cranberry juice, ginger ale, and a splash of lime juice.
Garnish: Sugared cranberries or a sprig of rosemary

- **Winter: Spiced Pear Fizz (Zero-Proof)**

A cozy and elegant blend of pear and spices
Recipe: Mix pear juice, ginger syrup, and sparkling water. Add a dash of nutmeg.
Garnish: Star anise or a thin pear slice

- **Winter: Pomegranate Mocktail (Zero-Proof)**

A tart and vibrant winter drink that feels celebratory
Recipe: Combine pomegranate juice, lime juice, and soda water over ice.
Garnish: Pomegranate seeds or a sprig of mint

Global Inspirations

- **Italy: Classic Aperol Spritz**

A bright and bittersweet Italian classic
Recipe: Combine equal parts Aperol, prosecco, and a splash of soda water over ice.
Garnish: Orange slice

- **Italy: Limonata with Basil (Zero-Proof)**

A citrusy Italian mocktail with a hint of herbal freshness
Recipe: Mix lemon juice, basil syrup, and soda water over ice.
Garnish: Fresh basil leaf

- **France: Kir Royale**

A sophisticated French cocktail with a hint of black currant
Recipe: Add crème de cassis to a champagne flute and top with sparkling wine.
Garnish: A fresh blackberry or lemon twist

- **France: French 75**

A crisp and citrusy champagne cocktail
Recipe: Combine gin, lemon juice, and simple syrup. Shake with ice, strain into a champagne flute, and top with sparkling wine.
Garnish: Lemon peel twist

- **Mexico: Paloma**

A refreshing tequila-based drink with a grapefruit twist
Recipe: Mix tequila, fresh grapefruit juice, lime juice, and soda water over ice. Add a pinch of salt.
Garnish: Grapefruit wedge or lime wheel

- **Mexico: Hibiscus Agua Fresca (Zero-Proof)**

A vibrant and tangy hibiscus tea-based refresher
Recipe: Brew dried hibiscus flowers with water and sweeten with simple syrup. Serve over ice.
Garnish: Lime wheel or fresh hibiscus flower

- **Nigeria: Chapman (Zero-Proof)**

A zesty, vibrant Nigerian classic
Recipe: Mix grenadine, Fanta, Sprite, and a splash of Angostura bitters. Add cucumber slices and ice.
Garnish: Cucumber wedge or orange slice

SIGNATURE COCKTAILS

Signature cocktails are a creative and memorable addition to any celebration. They reflect the event's theme and offer a personal touch, making your gathering truly special. When designing signature drinks, consider the season, location, and atmosphere. For summer picnics or outdoor events, lighter, refreshing cocktails or mocktails are ideal. For holiday parties, consider cozy, spiced options or festive flavors.

A signature cocktail doesn't need to be overly complicated! Start with a favorite spirit or flavor, add seasonal fruits or herbs, and finish with a unique garnish. Be sure to provide water stations for easy access, especially at outdoor events in warmer months.

bride

Creating Your Signature Cocktail

1. **Choose a base:** Begin with a spirit that resonates with the event's mood or holds personal meaning, like bourbon for a rustic gathering or gin for a botanical-themed celebration.
2. **Incorporate seasonal ingredients:** Fresh herbs, fruits, or spices that align with the season add depth and vibrancy. Local ingredients can enhance the freshness and create a memorable, localized touch.
3. **Select a distinctive garnish:** Elevate the visual appeal by adding seasonal or thematic garnishes—think edible flowers for spring, rosemary sprigs for winter, or sugared rims for a holiday feel.
4. **Create a memorable name:** Make it personal! A name like "The Blushing Bride" for a wedding or "Autumn Bliss" for a fall event adds meaning and whimsy, creating a connection to the occasion.
5. **Decorative ice cubes:** Decorative ice cubes, like floral-infused cubes, custom-carved designs, or textured patterns, add elegance and creativity to your drink presentation. They're a simple yet stunning detail that transforms cocktails and mocktails into unforgettable experiences.

Crafting a Unique and Memorable Drink Experience

Signature cocktails bring a unique personality to your celebration, offering guests a taste experience they'll remember long after the event. When creating a signature cocktail, consider the tone, location, and season; a refreshing citrus cocktail is perfect for a summer garden gathering, while a spiced whiskey cocktail brings warmth to a winter soiree.

DECORATIVE ICE CUBES: ELEVATE YOUR DRINK PRESENTATION

Decorative ice cubes are a simple yet stunning way to add a touch of elegance and creativity to your drink presentation. Whether you're serving signature cocktails or refreshing mocktails, the right ice can enhance not only the visual appeal but also the overall experience for your guests. With options like floral ice cubes, custom-carved designs, or patterned cubes, your drink station can become a conversation starter and an unforgettable detail of your celebration.

Types of Decorative Ice Cubes to Consider

- **Floral ice cubes:** Freeze edible flowers like pansies, roses, or lavender into crystal clear ice cubes for a romantic and whimsical touch. Perfect for garden parties or bridal showers, they add a pop of color and beauty to any drink.
- **Custom-carved ice cubes:** Work with a professional ice carver or use molds to create unique shapes that fit your theme—think monograms, hearts, or geometric designs. These elevate high-end cocktails and add a bespoke feel to your celebration.
- **Patterned ice cubes:** For a sleek and sophisticated touch, use clear ice cube molds and specialty stamps to create patterned cubes with elegant designs like diamond cuts, honeycomb patterns, or embossed logos. These add a modern, polished aesthetic to cocktails and mocktails, making them perfect for contemporary celebrations, whiskey tastings, or minimalist events. The clarity and intricate detailing of these ice cubes enhances the drink experience, proving that even the smallest details can leave a lasting impression.
- **Fruit ice cubes:** Fruit ice cubes are another delightful option, featuring frozen slices of citrus, berries, or herbs, adding both flavor and a vibrant pop of color to your drinks. **Pro Tip**: To achieve perfectly clear ice, use filtered or boiled water and freeze in layers for more intricate designs.

ARNOLD
Iced Tea

Decorative ice cubes are a simple yet impactful way to surprise and delight guests, proving that even the smallest details can elevate a drink experience. When thoughtfully designed, they enhance both the visual appeal and flavor profile, adding an extra layer of sophistication to every sip.

While it's fun to experiment with different ice designs, it's important to distinguish between purely decorative (nonedible) ice and edible ice that enhances the drink experience. Decorative elements like fruit, herbs, or edible flowers can add elegance and flavor, while additions—such as certain inks, dyes, or embedded objects—should be used with caution.

When styling drinks with decorative ice, always prioritize guest safety and comfort. A beautifully crafted cocktail should be as enjoyable to drink as it is to look at, so avoid serving ice with nonedible elements that could hinder the experience or pose a safety risk. Instead, opt for thoughtfully curated, edible additions that elevate the presentation while remaining functional and safe.

Whether it's floral-infused cubes for a garden party, fruit-filled ice for a refreshing summer cocktail, or custom-carved cubes for a modern event, these small but intentional touches bring a sense of artistry and elegance to your celebration.

DINNER

WINE SELECTIONS: WINE PAIRINGS BY COURSE AND MEAL

Pairing wine with food is a thoughtful way to enhance each course and create a cohesive dining experience.

Rosé

- An ideal pairing with charcuterie, light salads, or Mediterranean dishes, rosé's versatility makes it suitable for cocktail hours or brunches. Serve in a stemmed glass to maintain cool temperature.

Dessert Wine

- **Port or Sauternes:** Complements desserts with rich flavors, like chocolate cake, or pairs beautifully with cheese boards. Serve in small, narrow glasses to concentrate sweetness and aroma.
- Dessert wines are best served after the main meal, accompanying dessert or cheese, to conclude the dining experience elegantly.

White Wine

- **Chardonnay:** Pairs wonderfully with creamy dishes like chicken alfredo or lobster bisque. Best served in a rounded glass to concentrate aromas.
- **Sauvignon blanc:** Complements light, acidic dishes like salads, ceviche, or seafood. Serve in a smaller, tulip-shaped glass to retain its crisp aromas.

Red Wine

- **Cabernet sauvignon:** Perfect for hearty, rich dishes like steak or lamb. Use a large glass to allow for aeration.
- **Pinot noir:** Works well with lighter meats, salmon, or mushroom dishes. Serve in a wide-bowl glass to enhance aroma.

DINNER
MENU
SALAD COURSE
IRON SKILLET CORNBREAD
maple-honey butter
TRUFFLE PARMESAN BRIOCHE BREAD
HEIRLOOM TOMATO SALAD
watercress, toasted sweet potato
persian cucumber, soft feta cheese &
MAIN COURSE
FILET MIGNON
blackened asparagus

Choosing Glassware for Wine

- Red wines benefit from larger, rounded glasses, while white wines and rosés are best served in smaller, more compact glass shapes.
- Use narrower glasses for sparkling and dessert wines to preserve their bubbles and aromas.

Each wine, carefully selected and served in its ideal glassware, adds elegance and enhances the overall celebration, aligning with the meal's character and style.

750 ML
BRUT
12.5% ALC. VOL
Champagne

Glassware: Coupe vs. Flute

- **Champagne flute:** Its narrow shape preserves bubbles and is ideal for maintaining a festive look.
- **Coupe glass:** Known for its vintage appeal, the coupe allows a quicker release of bubbles and works well for champagne cocktails.

Zero-Proof Champagne

For an inclusive option, stock alcohol-free champagne, allowing guests who abstain to still partake in the celebratory toast without missing out on the experience.

CHAMPAGNE

Champagne Selections and Service

Champagne embodies the spirit of celebration, making it perfect for weddings, anniversaries, New Year's Eve, or milestone achievements. Its elegance suits formal events, while its lively bubbles add a festive touch to any occasion, from brunches to evening receptions.

TYPES AND ORIGINS

Champagne is exclusively from the Champagne region of France and includes various types:

- **Brut:** The driest and most common, perfect for toasts.
- **Extra brut:** Even drier than brut, ideal for pairing with rich appetizers.
- **Demi-sec:** Sweeter, suitable for dessert courses.

“

A THOUGHTFUL MENU CELEBRATES EVERYONE AT THE TABLE—MOCKTAILS SHOULDN'T BE AN AFTERTHOUGHT, BUT A REFLECTION OF INTENTIONAL, INCLUSIVE HOSPITALITY.

Signature
DRINKS
LOVE RUM PUNCH
Orange Juice
Pineapple Juice
Lime Juice
Rum
Grenadine

Have a drink on us
Have a drink on us
Have a drink on us

MOCKTAILS WITH IMPACT: RAISING THE BAR ON ZERO-PROOF COCKTAILS

Mocktails should not just be a side note—they're an essential part of creating an inclusive, memorable celebration experience. Offering flavorful, thoughtfully crafted nonalcoholic beverages ensure all guests, regardless of drinking preference, feel considered and included.

Crafting Memorable Mocktails

- **Seasonal ingredients:** Use fresh, seasonal produce like citrus in summer or spiced apple in winter to keep mocktails vibrant and celebratory.
- **Artistry in flavor:** Mixologists and bartenders work with nonalcoholic spirits, herbal infusions, and organic juices to create complex, layered flavors. Nonalcoholic spirits like Seedlip or Ritual help achieve the depth typically associated with cocktails, proving that zero-proof doesn't mean zero flavor.

Why Mocktails Matter

- **Inclusive celebrations:** Offering nonalcoholic options allows everyone—from designated drivers to guests with health considerations—to enjoy the ambiance fully.
- **Health-conscious choices:** Mocktails often contain fewer calories and support wellness goals, catering to guests who prioritize health without compromising on flavor.
- **Enhancing everyone's experience:** For major life events like weddings, mocktails add a sophisticated, inclusive element to toasts and drink stations. By providing quality nonalcoholic choices, you can enhance the experience and memories for all attendees.

Incorporating curated mocktails is a thoughtful way to welcome everyone to the celebration, proving that attention to detail at the bar can elevate any event's overall experience.

WATER

While water may seem like a simple detail, it's an essential part of the drink experience that often goes overlooked. Guests have varied preferences—some enjoy still, others sparkling, with or without lemon, and so on. Thoughtfully plan water options for each area of your event, from cocktail hour to the dinner table, to ensure it's readily available and accessible.

Consider elevating your water station with garnishes like cucumber slices, fresh mint, or citrus. By offering options and incorporating thoughtful touches, you create a refreshing and inclusive experience. Each water type adds a different experience to the event, so planning options to match your menu, theme, and guest preferences helps create a thoughtful, inclusive drink experience.

Reposado
Jalisco, Mexico
22.091
750 mL
GIN

Presentation Is Everything

Creating a visually appealing drink station is key to enhancing the guest experience. The right glassware—such as crystal clear tumblers, elegant coupes, or stemless wine glasses—brings sophistication to each sip, while thoughtful garnishes like rimmed salts, sugared rims, or artfully sliced fruit add flair. Fresh herbs, like rosemary or basil, offer aromatic hints and seasonal touches.

For drink stations, use stylish bar carts, trays, or accent tables to showcase your selection. Add small decorations, such as candles or floral accents, that complement the theme. Prepare garnishes in advance, matching them to seasonal ingredients for a festive touch. In summer, think citrus slices or edible flowers, while in winter, consider cinnamon sticks or sprigs of pine for a cozy vibe. Seasonal garnishes can beautifully enhance any occasion, adding visual appeal and a hint of seasonal flavor. These thoughtful, seasonal accents not only reflect the time of year but also provide guests with a sensory experience that complements each sip.

Selecting the Right Glassware for the Occasion:

Choosing the appropriate glassware adds sophistication to your drink presentation and enhances the guest experience. Here's a quick guide:

- **Wine glasses:** Use larger, rounded glasses for red wines to let flavors breathe, while serving white wines in slimmer, smaller glasses to preserve their crispness.
- **Champagne flutes:** The narrow flute retains bubbles, ideal for sparkling wines.
- **Cocktail glasses:** Martinis shine in classic stemmed glasses, while rocks glasses hold short, spirit-forward cocktails.
- **Highball glasses:** Perfect for tall, mixed drinks with ample mixers (like mojitos or gin and tonics).
- **Coupes:** A versatile, vintage option for champagne, cocktails, or even dessert presentations.
- **Water goblets:** Sturdy and generously sized, water goblets are perfect for serving still or sparkling water. Their versatile design complements any table setting, adding both practicality and elegance.

Selecting glassware tailored to each drink enhances both aesthetics and taste, elevating your celebration's overall feel.

MORE COCKTAILS PLEASE!

Specialty Cocktails
French Martini with a Twist
Pineapple juice, Chambord and vodka
Whiskey Smash Old Fashioned
Muddled lemon, mint, dash of simple syrup

EAT. DRINK & CELEBRATE.
AKIN's 0040 BIRTHDAY MISSION

Bar Accessories to Elevate Your Drink Experience

When it comes to a stylish bar setup, every detail counts. Every accessory—from napkins to signage—plays a role in crafting a memorable drink experience. These small touches may seem minor, but they add layers of personality and sophistication, making guests feel special with each sip. Think of cocktail napkins that match your theme, custom stirrers that spark conversation, and elegant signage that showcases your cocktail offerings with style.

When you bring intention to the drink selection and presentation, you're creating an experience that guests won't forget. Thoughtfully crafted signature drinks, paired with meaningful garnishes and intentional details, come together to elevate the entire celebration experience. As you raise a glass with your guests, you're toasting not only to the occasion itself but to the shared memories, laughter, and stories that make every gathering special. Here's to creating moments worth celebrating, one sip at a time. Cheers!

CURATING REFRESHING MOMENTS THAT RAISE THE BAR

Great drinks do more than quench thirst—they tell a story, complement the season, and bring people together. Use these ideas to craft an intentional beverage experience:

- **Offer a welcome drink:** Greet guests with a beverage that reflects your event's mood and sets the tone from the start.
- **Cater to all guests:** Include both cocktails and mocktails to make everyone feel seen and included.
- **Incorporate seasonal ingredients:** Use fresh herbs, fruits, and spices that highlight the flavors of the season.
- **Match your theme:** Choose drinks and garnishes that complement the aesthetic and tone of your celebration.
- **Elevate presentation:** Pair drinks with the proper glassware, stylish napkins, and thoughtful garnishes for a refined touch.
- **Hydration matters:** Don't forget still, sparkling, and infused water options to keep guests refreshed throughout the event.

CHAPTER 07

FLORAL DESIGN

Setting the Mood with Flowers.

Flowers have the remarkable ability to transform any space into a beautiful, memorable celebration. Whether you're designing a grand wedding or an intimate dinner party, flowers have a way of setting the tone, adding color, texture, and life to the occasion. In this chapter, we will explore how to create stunning floral arrangements that reflect the theme and mood of your celebration, and I'll share my personal journey into the world of floral design.

If you had told me fifteen years ago that I'd become known for my floral designs, I would have laughed. Back then, floral design was far outside my comfort zone.

My early experiences with design were centered on natural elements, like fabrics and textures, not fresh flowers. In fact, I used to shy away from flowers, viewing them as delicate and intimidating—something I could never handle for fear of breaking them. Fast forward to now, and I'm known for creating elaborate, over-the-top floral designs, not just on tables but at grand entrances and throughout entire event spaces. It's funny how things can change! Today, floral design is an essential part of my work. It's personal, creative, and even therapeutic. It's a way to express myself through art, and it allows me to connect with others in a profound way.

Key Aspects of Floral Design

Before we dive into specific techniques and styles, there are a few key elements to consider when starting your floral journey:

- **Flower selection:** Understanding which flowers work best for different seasons and themes is crucial. We'll explore seasonal flowers and how to choose blooms that complement your event's vibe.
- **Flower care:** Proper flower care is essential to ensuring your arrangements look fresh and beautiful for as long as possible. We'll cover tips for handling and caring for flowers, from cutting stems to keeping them hydrated.
- **Floral design styles and techniques:** Your floral design should reflect your style and the mood you wish to set. Whether you prefer classic or something more contemporary, there's no right or wrong way—only what feels true to you and your event.
- **Supplies:** You don't need a lot of fancy tools to start floral design, but there are some basic supplies that will make the process easier and more enjoyable. I'll walk you through the must-have tools to get started.

To me, floral design is more than simply arranging flowers—it's an art form, a way to artistically express beauty and emotion through petals, colors, and textures. I've come to appreciate that flowers aren't just fragile—they're resilient, versatile, and capable of telling a story. And when you understand how to work with them, floral design becomes not just less intimidating but also an exciting and deeply rewarding experience.

In this chapter, I want to demystify the world of floral design. We'll dive into floral care, design techniques, and how to develop your unique style. I know firsthand how intimidating it can seem at first, especially if you've never worked with flowers before. But once you begin to understand the basics and explore your creativity, floral design transforms into a fun, fulfilling, and deeply personal experience.

OVERCOMING FEAR AND FINDING YOUR STYLE

It's okay if floral design feels a little intimidating at first—it certainly was for me. But the key to mastering floral design is to embrace it as an art form that is personal and unique to you. There is no right or wrong way to arrange flowers; it's all about your creative vision. Don't be afraid to experiment and find your own style. Whether you prefer bold, dramatic arrangements or delicate, minimalistic designs, flowers offer endless possibilities to express yourself.

Tools for Foral Design

When working with flowers, having the right tools is essential to achieve both precision and creativity. Whether you're a seasoned professional or a beginner, these items will help you craft stunning arrangements:

- **¼–½ inch waterproof floral tape:** Essential for securing floral supplies like caging mechanisms and, in some cases, stems. It helps lock elements in place, ensuring stability and structure in intricate designs.
- **Floral shears:** These sharp shears are perfect for trimming stems to the desired length and creating clean cuts that help flowers absorb water.
- **Thorn remover:** A tool designed to strip thorns from roses and other thorny stems, making them easier to handle.
- **Floral pillow:** A reusable, eco-friendly alternative to floral foam, offering structural support and locking stems securely in place while allowing better hydration.
- **Spray bottle:** A gentle mist of water helps keep flowers fresh and hydrated, especially during the design process.
- **Vases**: The right vase can elevate your design. Choose shapes and sizes that complement your arrangements and the overall aesthetic of the event.
- **Floral buckets:** Essential for hydrating your flowers before arranging them. Always have clean, water-filled buckets on hand to keep stems fresh.
- **Lazy Susan or turntable:** A 14" tabletop Lazy Susan is an invaluable tool for floral design, allowing you to rotate your vase and get a 360-degree view as you arrange your flowers. This ensures balance, symmetry, and a well-rounded design from every angle.

FLOWER SELECTION

Choosing the right flowers is a crucial part of the floral design process. I like to break my selections into four main categories, each playing a distinct role in the overall arrangement.

Four Main Categories

1. **The base:** These are foundational flowers or greenery that create structure and support for your arrangement. Examples include hydrangeas, eucalyptus, and Italian ruscus.
2. **Fillers:** Fillers are smaller blooms or foliage that add volume and texture, creating depth in the arrangement. Examples include baby's breath and wax flower.
3. **Feature flowers:** These are the focal points of your design, typically using two to three standout varieties that draw attention and set the tone for the arrangement. Examples include standard roses, garden roses, dahlias, and peonies.
4. **Accent flowers:** These delicate or unique blooms add personality, charm, and contrast, helping to tie everything together. Examples include orchids, spray roses, ranunculus, berries, and sweet peas.

“

BY CATEGORIZING YOUR FLOWERS, YOU CAN ENSURE THAT YOUR ARRANGEMENT FEELS BALANCED, VISUALLY INTERESTING, AND COHESIVE WITH YOUR EVENT'S THEME AND MOOD.

Floral Care and Prep

One of the first lessons I learned when I started designing flowers was that the beauty of a centerpiece depends on proper floral care. No matter how stunning your arrangement is, if the flowers aren't well prepared, they won't last throughout your celebration. The key to longevity is in the details—hydration, conditioning, and handling with care. Before you start designing, follow these essential steps to ensure your flowers remain fresh and vibrant for as long as possible.

- **Clean stems:** Clean stems are essential for a healthy arrangement. Begin by grabbing a clean bucket of room-temperature water. Strip the leaves from the stems to prevent any foliage from sitting in the water, which could promote bacteria growth.
- **Trim the stems:** Trim ¼ inch off the bottom of each stem. This opens a fresh source for the flower to absorb water and stay hydrated.
- **Hydrate the flowers:** Once your stems are prepared, allow them to hydrate for a little while—especially if they've been out of water for an extended period. For flowers that have been out for a long time, let them sit in water for at least one or two hours before you start designing.

By incorporating these elements, you'll create an event that feels deeply personal and resonates with both you and your guests.

STEPS FOR DESIGNING A STANDARD CENTERPIECE

1. **Prep your vase:** While the flowers hydrate, clean your vase with water.
2. **Caging mechanism:** Secure the cage on top of the vase with waterproof floral tape to hold flowers in place.
3. **Add water:** Fill the vase with fresh water, ensuring it's at the right level to keep your flowers hydrated without spilling.
4. **Start with base flowers:** Use base flowers like hydrangeas to frame the shape and determine the height and width of the arrangement. Keep the table or area in mind when deciding on size and flow, ensuring it enhances the table without distracting from the overall atmosphere.
5. **Add fillers for volume and texture:** Once the base shape is established, incorporate fillers such as greenery or smaller blooms to create depth and dimension. Use them strategically to conceal any mechanics like floral tape or caging, ensuring a seamless look. However, avoid overcrowding—leave enough space for your feature flowers to stand out beautifully.
6. **Incorporate feature flowers:** Place your feature flowers (roses, peonies, dahlias) in prominent positions. These flowers should stand out as the centerpiece's focal point, showcasing their beauty without being hidden by other flowers.
7. **Add accent flowers:** After the main flowers are in, go around the arrangement with accent flowers like orchids or spray roses. These should not be hidden but should subtly pop out, adding contrast and charm to the centerpiece.
8. **Finish with a spray:** Once the arrangement is complete, give it a light mist with water to keep everything fresh and hydrated.
9. **Repurpose loose stems in bud vases:** For any leftover or broken stems, place them in small bud vases. These can be scattered around the event space or used as complementary decor, ensuring nothing goes to waste.

GETTING THE MOST OUT OF YOUR FLOWERS

- **Handle carefully:** Always hold flowers by the stem to avoid bruising or damaging the petals.
- **Prep roses:** Remove the outer petals of roses that may look brown or damaged to reveal the vibrant inner layers.
- **Keep cool:** Store flowers in a cool, dry place, away from direct sunlight or heat sources.
- **Quick-dip hydration:** For extra hydration, dip freshly cut stems into a quick-dip solution before arranging them.
- **Maintain hydration:** Make sure your flowers are continuously hydrated, especially for longer events.

This should be the same approach for you. Your floral design should be a reflection of your personal style and the mood you wish to create for your celebration. Thoughtfully designed florals have the power to set the tone, evoke emotions, and encourage connection among your guests.

Whether you gravitate toward classic, romantic arrangements with soft, cascading blooms; modern and structured designs with clean lines; or bold, artistic compositions that push creative boundaries; there's no right or wrong way to approach floral design—only what feels true to you and your vision.

Trust your instincts, experiment, and, most importantly, have fun with it. Your floral choices should enhance the experience, leaving a lasting impression on everyone who gathers around them.

FLORAL DESIGN STYLES AND TECHNIQUES

The fun part about floral design is finding your own style. As a designer, this was key for me. Over the years, I've found myself drawn to a romantic, layered floral aesthetic—one that feels lush, intentional, and full of movement. It's a style that has become synonymous with my work, something my clients love and seek out in my designs. I approach every arrangement as a form of storytelling, crafting florals that not only enhance a space but also create an emotional connection. Whether I'm designing for a personal gathering or a large-scale event, florals are always at the heart of the experience.

To guide you through this creative process, here are a few popular design styles:

- **Classic and timeless:** Think symmetry, soft color palettes, and traditional blooms like roses, hydrangeas, and peonies. These arrangements tend to have a romantic, formal feel, perfect for weddings, anniversaries, or more elegant events. A classic design emphasizes structure and balance, with each element thoughtfully placed to achieve a sense of harmony.
- **Modern and minimalist:** If you prefer clean lines and understated elegance, a modern design style may be your preference. In this approach, less is more—think monochromatic palettes or a focus on a single variety of flower, like orchids or tulips. The emphasis is on negative space and simplicity, allowing the natural beauty of the flowers to shine.
- **Whimsical and free-form:** For a more relaxed and organic vibe, consider a whimsical or free-form style. These arrangements often have an asymmetrical design, with a mix of unexpected flowers, textures, and wild greenery. Play with heights, colors, and different flower varieties to create something playful and dynamic.
- **Rustic and natural:** Rustic floral design often incorporates elements from nature—branches, wood, wildflowers, and lots of greenery. This style is perfect for outdoor celebrations or events with a cozy, earthy vibe. Sunflowers, lavender, and wild blooms are commonly used to achieve this aesthetic.
- **Bold and eclectic:** For those who love color and want their florals to make a statement, the bold and eclectic style is perfect. This approach mixes vibrant hues and a variety of flower types for an eye-catching, layered effect. You can incorporate unexpected elements, such as fruits or exotic flowers, to create a truly one-of-akind arrangement.

Designing with your personal style and the specific mood you wish to create will ensure your florals are not only beautiful but also meaningful and unique to your event.

No matter which style you choose, remember that floral design is about self-expression. Play with colors, textures, and shapes until you create something that feels like an extension of your personality and the celebration you're hosting.

CREATING YOUR OWN DESIGN AND SIGNATURE STYLE

Developing your signature style in floral design takes time, exploration, and a personal connection to the craft. The process begins with getting to know yourself as a designer. Spend time observing what inspires you—whether it's nature, colors, textures, or even specific types of flowers.

Tips for Cultivating Your Creative Techniques and Style

- **Self-reflection:** Set aside a day for self-reflection. Use a journal or notebook to note what catches your eye or sparks your joy as you go about your day. Are you drawn to certain flowers, colors, or textures? Take pictures on your phone or clip out images that inspire you, and jot down thoughts or ideas that resonate.
- **Experiment and play:** Don't feel confined by traditional rules or structures. Let your creativity guide you—experiment with different arrangements, colors, and combinations. Put on some music, pour a glass of wine, and create in a space that feels free and joyful. This is your moment to express your personal style through flowers.
- **Recognize your repetition:** As you continue to design, take note of the patterns and choices you tend to make repeatedly. This could be a particular way you arrange stems, the types of flowers you use, or the color palettes you gravitate toward. Recognizing these behaviors will help you discover and refine your unique style.

FLORAL DESIGN IS MORE THAN JUST FOLLOWING STEPS—IT'S AN ART FORM, A MEANS OF PERSONAL EXPRESSION, AND A WAY TO CONNECT WITH YOUR GUESTS ON A DEEPER LEVEL.

Allow yourself the freedom to explore, create, and bring joy through your arrangements. By choosing blooms that resonate with the event's theme, caring for them properly, and arranging them with intention, you create an atmosphere that will linger in your guests' memories long after the celebration ends.

Remember, floral design is as much about artistry as it is about emotion. Every petal, arrangement, and detail is an opportunity to communicate beauty, joy, and connection. Whether you're crafting a centerpiece or adding small touches here and there, let your creativity and passion shine. Embrace the journey of floral design as an expression of who you are and the love you bring to each celebration.

DESIGNING WITH INTENTION, TEXTURE, AND EMOTION

Florals are more than decor—they're storytellers. From centerpieces to subtle accents, each bloom adds depth, beauty, and emotion to your event. Use these notes to guide your floral planning:

- **Select with purpose:** Choose flowers that reflect the event's theme, season, and overall mood.
- **Prep your blooms:** Trim stems, remove leaves below the waterline, and hydrate flowers before arranging to ensure freshness.
- **Gather your tools:** Have floral shears, tape, foam, buckets, and containers ready for seamless design execution.
- **Balance and proportion matter:** Create visual flow by mixing focal blooms with supporting elements in a balanced way.
- **Layer textures and heights:** Blend lush florals, greenery, and fillers to create dimension—and play with height while maintaining guest visibility.
- **Use every bloom:** Repurpose leftovers in bud vases or accent areas like restrooms and entryways for a cohesive feel.
- **Experiment with color:** Whether soft and tonal or bold and unexpected, color palettes can transform a space and mood.
- **Consider a floral collaborator:** For largerscale events or elevated arrangements, working with a florist can bring your vision to life while allowing you to enjoy the process.

CHAPTER 08

TABLE SETTING

Designing a Beautiful Tablescape.

The table has always been a gathering place—a space where meals are shared, stories unfold, and time slows down. Creating a beautiful tablescape is essential for all celebrations. It's not just about placing plates and glasses—it's about setting the stage for memories to be made. In this chapter, we'll explore how to design a table setting that not only complements the theme and mood of your event but also enhances the overall experience for your guests.

The table is more than just a place to dine—it's a timeless space of togetherness. It's where guests linger, conversations unfold, and memories quietly take shape. When thoughtfully set, the table becomes a stage for connection, where the beauty of the setting enhances the experience of sharing food, laughter, and meaningful moments. It's where intentional design meets heartfelt purpose, and every detail invites a sense of belonging, comfort, and joy.

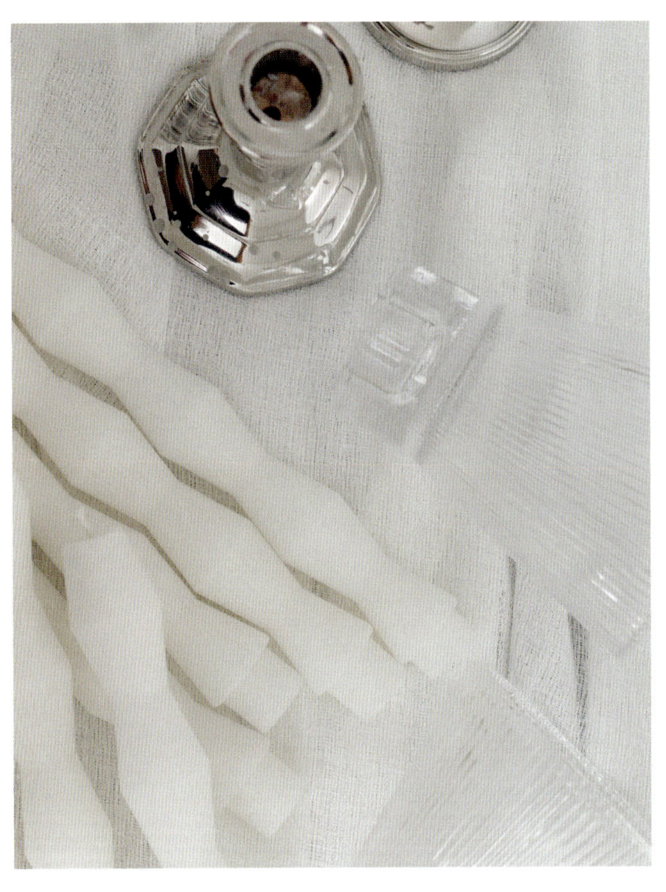

GATHER AROUND

Across cultures and generations, the table remains a sacred space—where traditions are honored and new stories begin. As a child, I vividly remember the excitement of pulling out the special china, glassware, napkins, and all the beautiful items that would grace the table when we had special guests visiting. I can still picture where my mom hid the key to the "good stuff"—it's funny how those small details stay with you over the years. Her prized blue china, with its intricate patterns and delicate etchings, left an impression on me that time hasn't erased. Even today, years after her passing, that same china remains tucked away in two of our family homes—one in the village of Okpella, where my family would spend our holidays, and the other in our childhood home in Benin City.

Each plate, each piece of glassware, and each linen napkin carried meaning. They weren't just items on a table; they were symbols of care, thoughtfulness, and the importance of gathering together. These details taught me that a beautifully set table does more than just provide a place to sit—it creates an atmosphere of celebration, warmth, and connection. Today, I carry that sense of excitement in my personal celebrations and for my clients.

“

EVERY TABLE YOU DESIGN IS AN OPPORTUNITY TO CREATE MAGIC—A SPACE WHERE BEAUTY, CONNECTION, AND UNFORGETTABLE MEMORIES COME TO LIFE.

The Power of a Tablescape

Looking back, it wasn't just the china that made those moments special; it was the sense of togetherness and celebration that filled the room. Whether it was a birthday, a wedding, or even a funeral, our family gatherings always revolved around the table. There was a certain magic that came to life when we gathered, even if the house was packed and filled with noise. I miss those moments, and I miss her—my mom. But what my family gifted me is the joy of celebrating life through these gatherings.

Over the years, I've developed a signature style for tablescape design, which almost always includes flowers. Floral arrangements have an incredible way of telling a story and adding the perfect finishing touch to any table. Whether your centerpiece consists of lush blooms, flickering candles, or unexpected elements like fruit, let your creativity and inspiration guide you. The key is to ensure every detail aligns with the story you're crafting for your celebration, making the experience both visually stunning and deeply meaningful.

My hope is that after reading this chapter, you'll feel inspired to approach your next tablescape with the same sense of excitement and joy.

Designing the Perfect Tablescape

Setting a table goes far beyond simply arranging plates and glasses—it's about telling a story and creating a cohesive experience that mirrors the mood, theme, and tone of your event. I've noticed that many people feel intimidated by the idea of setting the perfect tablescape, and I get it—it can seem daunting. But this chapter is here to change that perspective. I want you to look at the art of creating a beautiful tablescape with excitement and joy, not fear. Believe me, you can do this!

By the end of this chapter, it is my hope that you'll feel confident and inspired to create a tablescape that not only looks beautiful but also tells a story your guests will remember. Let's dive into the art of setting a table and creating a tablescape that will not only wow your guests but also set the tone for a memorable celebration.

Choosing and Coordinating Colors

1. **Pick a primary color:** Start with a dominant color that reflects the heart of your event's theme. This color will serve as the foundation, appearing in larger elements like tablecloths or primary centerpieces.
2. **Add complementary colors:** Choose one or two complementary colors that enhance your primary shade. These will appear in accents, such as napkins, glassware, or small decor items. Use a color wheel if you're unsure of combinations—shades across from each other on the wheel often work well together.
3. **Layer textures for depth:** Don't just rely on color—textures play a significant role in creating visual interest. For instance, pair smooth satin napkins with a textured linen tablecloth, or mix matte and glossy finishes in your glassware and dinnerware. This layering adds richness to your table without overwhelming the color scheme.
4. **Use neutral tones as anchors:** Incorporating neutrals like white, beige, or soft gray provides balance and prevents bold colors from feeling overpowering. Neutrals work beautifully as a backdrop for vibrant blooms, colorful glassware, or patterned plates.

SELECT A COHESIVE COLOR PALETTE

A well-chosen color palette can transform your tablescape into an immersive experience that aligns with your celebration's theme. Color is powerful—it sets the mood, enhances the atmosphere, and ties every element of your decor together. When selecting colors, consider the season, the setting, and the tone you want to convey. For example, soft pastels and neutrals work beautifully for spring gatherings, while rich jewel tones or deep greens bring warmth to autumn and winter celebrations.

Creating a Visual Flow

When putting your palette into action, arrange colors so they flow harmoniously from one element to another. For instance, a soft gradient effect with your floral arrangements or a subtle ombré effect with candles can help lead the eye naturally across the table. Balance bold accents with softer hues, ensuring each element supports the next.

By carefully selecting colors and textures that align with your event's vision, you create a cohesive and polished tablescape that feels inviting, intentional, and utterly unforgettable.

INCORPORATING COLOR AND TEXTURE

Color and texture add depth, vibrancy, and a touch of the unexpected, creating a sensory experience that can transform an ordinary table into something truly captivating. Growing up, I spent countless hours in my mom's tailoring shop, fascinated by the bold colors and rich textures of the fabric bolts stacked around me. That early exposure to textiles shaped my approach to table design today. I still own a sewing machine, and if I can't find the perfect linen or texture for a tablescape, I'll source the fabric myself and sew it to match the vision.

HE ART OF
LEBRATING
DECOR & PLANNING
Drink recipes perfect for spring and summer entertaining
Tips for designing beautiful spring flower arrangements
Inspiration for your easter brunch tablescape
SPRING INTO LOVE
10 EASY WAYS TO UPGRADE YOUR HOME FOR SPRING
PLUS
HOW TO PUT TOGETHER THE ULTIMATE SPRING/SUMMER WARDROBE
THE GRATITUDE ISSUE
TRANSITION IN STYLE
PLUS
FALL ENTERTAINING GUIDE

Table Linens and Napkins

One of the first things I notice when sitting at a table is the linen—the feel of a good quality cloth, the texture of a detailed napkin. Linens are an incredibly powerful tool in setting the mood and bringing personality to a table. They can be a simple way to introduce color, a touch of luxury, or a theme into your design. Whether it's an elegant velvet tablecloth, a crisp linen napkin, or a playfully patterned runner, each piece can add a layer of visual interest.

A beautifully textured table linen or a monogrammed napkin can add a layer of sophistication and tie the entire theme together. Don't overlook these details—they may seem small, but they make a big impact. Be sure to keep a few extra napkins on hand for unexpected needs, and don't forget about the bread basket napkins to maintain a polished presentation.

Tips for Selecting Linens and Napkins

- **Choose textures that complement the season and theme:** Use soft, airy linens for spring and summer events, and opt for heavier fabrics like velvet or brocade in the colder months.
- **Play with color and patterns:** Don't be afraid to introduce bold colors or patterns in small doses. A patterned table runner or brightly colored napkins can make a subtle, sophisticated statement.
- **Mix linens for a unique look:** You don't have to use the same linen material for both the table and napkins. Mixing linens keeps the look interesting and dynamic, adding layers of texture without overwhelming the table.
- **Incorporate fun napkin rings or folds:** Napkin rings and creative napkin folds add personality to the table. Go for textures like hammered metal or wood for a rustic feel or sparkling crystal for a touch of glamour.

LAYERING ELEMENTS

Layering elements on your table is an artful way to add visual depth and create a dynamic, inviting tablescape. By carefully layering linens, plates, and glassware, you can build an experience that feels both polished and welcoming. Each layer offers an opportunity to introduce texture, color, and personality, allowing every piece to tell its own story while harmonizing with the overall look.

Steps for Effective Layering

1. **Start with the foundation:** Begin with a tablecloth or table runner that complements your theme, either with a bold pattern, a rich texture, or a soft, neutral hue that sets the stage for other layers. Consider adding a second, thinner runner down the center for added contrast.
2. **Add chargers for structure:** Charger plates serve as both a visual anchor and a functional base for the dinnerware. Select chargers in materials or colors that either contrast or coordinate with the tablecloth, creating a frame around each place setting that draws attention.
3. **Play with plate sizes and styles:** Stack different plate sizes—such as a dinner plate, salad plate, and appetizer plate—to add height and interest. For an eclectic look, mix patterns or colors, but ensure they complement each other to avoid a chaotic feel.
4. **Incorporate layers of texture:** Use textured napkins, fabric place mats, or even table mats to introduce layers that add both softness and depth. Choose linen, velvet, or woven fabrics to create a tactile experience that feels inviting.
5. **Finish with glassware and flatware:** Vary the heights and styles of your glassware, mixing stemmed glasses with shorter tumblers. Similarly, use unique flatware finishes, such as matte or hammered metal, to add visual complexity and style.

- **Mixed metals and unique finishes:** Incorporating different metals can add a modern, eclectic touch to your table. Think about using gold flatware with silver chargers or copper napkin rings with glass plates.

- **Textured glassware and flatware:** Hammered or tinted glassware, as well as patterned flatware, can subtly introduce color while providing a tactile experience for guests. For instance, choosing vintage-inspired glassware or tinted goblets can create a beautiful contrast against classic white plates.

- **Candles and vases for additional color and texture:** Candleholders and vases offer another opportunity to play with color and texture. A mix of glass, metal, or ceramic candleholders in varying heights creates a layered, visually interesting centerpiece. Vases in complementary colors or textures can further tie together the tablescape's design.

Mixing Materials

Another way I introduce color and texture in my tablescapes is through the careful selection of other table elements, from floral arrangements to glassware and flatware. This approach helps me visualize a cohesive color story and ensures that every layer adds to the theme rather than distracting from it.

ELEVATING THE EXPERIENCE WITH DINNERWARE

Designing the culinary aspect of an event goes beyond the food—it's about crafting an unforgettable experience. The presentation of your food and drinks should match the level of effort you've put into planning the menu. The right dinnerware can make all the difference in elevating the guest experience. From passed hors d'oeuvres to seated dinners, interactive food stations to dessert tables, each element should feel cohesive and thoughtfully chosen.

One of my personal joys is exploring antique shops for unique, vintage tableware. Over the years, I've curated a beautiful collection, from delicate wine glasses to exquisite plates, serving trays and more. It's an incredibly rewarding pursuit, adding character and a timeless charm to my events.

Charger Plates

Charger plates, or service plates, form the foundation of a place setting, providing an elegant base for each course. They're placed beneath the dinner plates and help retain heat while also adding an extra layer of style and protection to the table linens. Chargers come in various colors, materials, and shapes, allowing you to infuse personality and creativity into your tablescape.

Pro Tip: *Place chargers about one inch from the edge of the table, with roughly two feet between guests for comfort. Remember, chargers are removed before dessert to keep the setting clean and uncluttered.*

Dinner Plates

From the main course plate to bread, butter, soup, and salad plates, each piece should reflect your style and the tone of your celebration. A quality dinnerware set can serve as an anchor through many celebrations and seasons, making each meal feel distinctive yet familiar.

Choosing dinnerware allows for a delightful play with colors, patterns, shapes, and even textures. Consider plates with subtle patterns for a timeless feel or bold hues for a more dramatic effect. Your dinnerware should feel both beautiful and functional, making it a joy to set the table and a pleasure for your guests to enjoy their meal.

Dinnerware

Selecting the right dinnerware is essential for creating a polished and cohesive dining experience. From salad plates and entrée dishes to dessert plates, each piece plays a role in enhancing the presentation of your menu. Opting for a matching set provides a refined and harmonious look, while mixing patterns, textures, or colors can add personality and visual interest to your table. I especially love incorporating a combination of unique plates to bring character and depth to the tablescape, making each setting feel intentional and thoughtfully curated.

CENTERPIECES AND DECOR

The centerpiece is the focal point of the tablescape, creating visual interest and enhancing the atmosphere of your event. It's not just about flowers or candles; the centerpiece sets the tone for the gathering, bringing together elements of color, texture, and theme. A thoughtfully crafted centerpiece invites guests to feel connected, adding layers of beauty without overwhelming the table.

Balancing Height and Visual Flow

The balance of height is key in centerpiece design. Tall arrangements create drama, while lower elements keep the line of sight open for conversation. Alternating tall and low arrangements or incorporating candles of varying heights can give the table a dynamic look while maintaining balance.

Tips for Balancing Height and Flow

- **Alternate high and low elements:** On longer tables, vary the height of floral arrangements, candlesticks, or lanterns to create a cascading effect.
- **Consider line of sight:** Keep arrangements under twelve inches or above twenty-four inches if you want guests to have an unobstructed view across the table.
- **Add small accents:** Scatter small vases, single-bloom bud vases, or small candles around larger centerpieces to add continuity without overcrowding.

Michelle
Molly
Merlyn
Rob
Amy

Final Touches

The finishing touches can bring your centerpiece to life. A gentle spritz of water to fresh flowers, a quick polish to crystal elements, or ensuring each candle is perfectly straight—all of these details make a difference. Once everything is in place, step back and assess the overall look, making any adjustments to ensure it feels cohesive and balanced.

By thoughtfully designing your centerpieces and incorporating decor elements that align with your event's theme and mood, you create a tablescape that's not just visually pleasing but deeply memorable. Let each piece tell a story, inviting your guests into a celebration of beauty, connection, and warmth.

SETTING THE TABLE FOR SEAMLESS FLOW

Arranging each element with intention ensures that the table flows naturally, allowing guests to fully enjoy the experience without distraction. Every component—from plates and glasses to floral arrangements and decor—should work in harmony to create a balanced, inviting, and cohesive look. Thoughtful arrangement enhances not only the visual appeal but also the functionality of the setting, encouraging guests to comfortably interact with each other and the elements on the table.

When it comes to arranging everything, it's best to follow a step-by-step approach:

1. **Start with the foundation:** Begin by ensuring the table itself is sturdy, stable, and well suited for the size of your gathering. This may seem obvious, but a solid base is essential for a seamless dining experience.
2. **Lay the linens**: Next, set down your tablecloth, runner, or place mats. Linens create the backdrop for your tablescape, adding color, texture, and style. Smooth out any creases and ensure they are aligned properly.
3. **Add centerpieces and decor:** Once your linens are in place, position your centerpiece, candles, and any decorative elements. It's best to arrange centerpieces first, so you can visualize how the rest of the table will come together without obstructing view lines across the table.
4. **Set the plates and chargers:** Position chargers or base plates around the table, aligning each plate about one inch from the edge for uniformity. Place dinner plates on top of chargers, followed by appetizer or salad plates if they're part of the meal.

THE ART OF TABLE SETTING IS ABOUT CRAFTING A SPACE WHERE EVERYONE FEELS WELCOME—A PLACE WHERE MEMORIES ARE MADE AND CELEBRATIONS COME ALIVE.

5. **Arrange the flatware:** Place flatware in the order it will be used, working from the outside in. Forks go to the left of the plate, and knives and spoons go on the right. ' place knives with the blades facing inward, toward the plate, for safety and etiquette.
6. **Position glassware:** Place water glasses directly above the knives, with wine glasses positioned slightly to the right and above the water glass. This makes it easy for guests to reach for their drinks without crowding the plate.
7. **Finalize with napkins and place cards:** Napkins can be folded and placed on top of plates or set to the left of the forks for a traditional look. Personalize each setting by adding place cards to create a welcoming touch.
8. **Refine with symmetry:** Step back and view your table from different angles to ensure everything is symmetrical and aligned. Adjust any plates, glassware, or decor that may be slightly out of place to keep the setting balanced and visually appealing.
9. **Final check for functionality:** Make sure there is enough space for guests to dine comfortably without knocking over glasses or brushing against centerpieces. Clear any excess items or distractions that might interfere with the dining experience, ensuring everything feels purposeful.
10. **Step back and enjoy:** Finally, step back one last time and admire your work. Take in the complete picture of your tablescape to ensure it reflects the theme and mood you envisioned, with every detail in place to create a cohesive and inviting atmosphere.

As we've explored in this chapter, a thoughtfully designed tablescape is more than just a setting—it's a canvas for creating cherished memories. Every item you place, from the plates and glassware to the centerpieces and personalized touches, contributes to a unique experience that your guests will carry with them. Remember, it's not about perfection but about intention and warmth. When you set the table with love and care, you invite others to feel at home, to connect, and to share in the beauty of the occasion.

In the end, the art of table setting is about crafting a space where everyone feels welcome—a place where memories are made and celebrations come alive. Embrace each gathering as an opportunity to share a piece of your heart, and let your tablescape be a reflection of your unique style and passion for bringing people together.

LAYERING STYLE, FUNCTION, AND HEART AT THE TABLE

The table is where conversation flows, memories are made, and every detail counts. Use this guide to design a tablescape that's as inviting as it is intentional:

- **Set a cohesive vision:** Choose a theme and color palette that carries through your linens, place settings, florals, and decor.
- **Keep form and function in balance:** Ensure guests have enough room to dine comfortably, and that centerpieces don't obstruct sightlines or disrupt the dining experience.
- **Infuse personal touches:** Incorporate custom place cards, personalized menus, or thoughtful favors to create a warm, meaningful atmosphere.
- **Play with layers and textures:** Combine materials—like soft linens, patterned chargers, and sleek glassware—to add dimension and elevate the visual experience.
- **Mind the height:** Mix tall and low elements in your centerpiece design, but prioritize guest connection and visibility.
- **Use lighting to set the tone:** Candles, twinkle lights, or statement lighting pieces create ambiance and elevate the mood.
- **Craft cohesive settings:** Align plates, utensils, and glasses with precision for a refined and welcoming presentation.
- **Celebrate the season:** Tie in seasonal blooms, produce, or tones to ground your design in the moment and create a sense of occasion.

CHAPTER 09

MUSIC

Setting the Tone for the Celebration.

Music is the universal language of emotion. It's one of the most powerful ways to set the tone of a celebration, creating an ambiance that influences the mood, energy, and flow of your event. From soft, welcoming tunes as guests arrive to lively beats that get everyone on the dance floor, music is a thread that ties your celebration together.

One of the most exciting aspects of planning a celebration is curating the entertainment. There are so many fun and creative ways to incorporate music into an event, making this process one of my favorite parts of planning.

In my approach to designing the guest experience, I carefully consider how music will set the stage for each moment, transitioning seamlessly from one experience to the next. Whether it's a live band playing during an intimate dinner, an upbeat DJ set keeping the energy high, or a surprise performance that captivates the crowd, music is never an afterthought—it's a key part of the overall experience.

Setting the Tone for the Celebration

THE ROLE OF MUSIC IN CELEBRATIONS

Music influences how we feel, interact, and remember special occasions. It complements every element of your event, from the food and decor to the overall vibe. Think of music as your silent host, guiding the experience while adding depth to every moment.

When planning your event's music, start with the mood and vibe you want to create. Ask yourself:

- ***What emotions do I want guests to feel when they arrive?***
- ***How should the music shift as the event progresses?***
- ***What's the overall energy I want to leave guests with?***

Personalizing your music selection also adds a layer of intimacy to your celebration. Ask your guests for song requests beforehand, incorporating tracks that resonate with their memories and preferences. Hearing a favorite song can evoke nostalgia and strengthen connections, making the event feel special.

In this chapter, we'll explore how to use music thoughtfully to enhance your event, from choosing the right soundtrack to creating unforgettable moments through sound. Whether played at a casual gathering, an elegant dinner, or a lavish celebration, music has the ability to evoke emotions, connect people, and elevate the experience.

THE MOMENT GUESTS STEP INTO YOUR EVENT, MUSIC SHOULD GREET THEM WARMLY.

CURATING THE MUSICAL JOURNEY

Light, upbeat tunes like acoustic melodies, jazz, or soft pop create a welcoming and positive atmosphere. These sounds should complement the event's theme, allowing guests to feel at ease as they mingle and settle in.

For me, one of the most exciting parts of planning an event is curating an immersive musical experience—one that connects guests to the location, culture, and overall theme of the celebration. I love incorporating local entertainment into destination events to enhance the atmosphere and create an authentic sense of place.

At a Paris wedding celebration, we designed a Parisian-inspired entertainment experience for the welcome party. Guests were greeted by lively cabaret dancers and greeters dressed in chic Parisian attire, setting the tone for the evening. A live Parisian band played classic French melodies while cabaret-style performances popped up throughout the night, transporting guests straight to the heart of Paris.

For a celebration in Mexico, the welcome party was a full sensory experience. We curated an evening filled with traditional mariachi music, a genre deeply rooted in Mexican culture, blending seamlessly with salsa dancers who encouraged guests to join in the rhythm of the night. As the evening unfolded, fire dancers captivated the crowd with their electrifying performance, and the night ended with an unforgettable DJ set, keeping the energy high well into the night.

As guests take their seats for dinner, the energy should naturally shift to something softer and more intimate. Instrumental pieces, classical arrangements, or soft vocal tracks maintain a relaxed ambiance, allowing for seamless conversation and a refined dining experience. Thoughtful music transitions during this portion of the evening ensure that guests remain engaged and comfortable.

Once dinner is over, it's time to raise the energy with a lively mix of timeless classics, modern hits, and curated tracks that reflect the event's unique vibe. Whether it's a blend of old-school funk, contemporary pop, or cultural rhythms tied to the location, the playlist should inspire guests to hit the dance floor. For an added wow factor, a surprise live performance—such as a saxophonist accompanying the DJ, an energetic dance act, or a percussionist playing alongside the beats—can elevate the excitement and make the celebration unforgettable.

As a planner and event producer, I believe music should be deeply woven into every element of the event, aligning perfectly with immersive experiences like live performances, surprise acts, and even fireworks displays.

For grand finales, we've timed firework displays to the beat of the song selections, creating an unforgettable crescendo that leaves guests in awe. At wedding celebrations, we've coordinated live instrumentalists—like saxophonists or electric violinists—to play alongside DJs, adding an unexpected thrill to the dance floor. At afterparties, we've introduced interactive drummers or percussionists, heightening the energy and creating a club-like atmosphere.

MUSIC IS MORE THAN JUST BACKGROUND NOISE; IT SETS THE TONE FOR THE CELEBRATION.

These well-timed, music-driven moments are what make celebrations feel larger than life. When thoughtfully executed, music transforms from being just an ambiance enhancer to a powerful storytelling tool, guiding guests through an emotional and unforgettable journey from the first song to the very last note.

At the end of the day, music is more than just a background element—it's an experience, an emotion, and a way to create a lasting impression on your guests. When thoughtfully curated, it ensures that every moment of your celebration flows seamlessly and leaves a mark that lingers long after the last song fades.

Surprise and Delight

Music is an incredible tool for creating unexpected moments of magic at your event. Imagine a live band emerging during dessert, a harpist setting the tone during dinner, or strolling musicians, synchronized swimmers, or a string quartet surprising guests at cocktail hour.

A common misconception is that live performances or curated musical experiences are reserved for grand celebrations like weddings. In reality, even a small gathering can be transformed with an immersive musical moment—whether it's a solo guitarist at an intimate dinner or an acoustic singer welcoming guests to a birthday celebration.

When curating my celebrations, I love incorporating unexpected entertainment experiences at key moments to enhance the energy and ambiance. There's something magical about arriving at a venue and being instantly serenaded by live music or immersive entertainment—from a saxophonist setting the mood to staggered violinists, ballerina dancers, or a dynamic live ensemble. For weddings, I often integrate entertainment seamlessly, using music to guide guests through transitions, from arrival to ceremony and beyond. Entertainment should be more than just a performance; it should transport guests into the experience you're creating, making every moment feel like a beautiful escape into celebration.

ENHANCING THE CELEBRATION BEYOND MUSIC

While music is undeniably a powerful tool for setting the tone of any celebration, there are many other interactive and immersive experiences that can elevate the guest experience. Incorporating nonmusical entertainment elements such as live painters, cigar rollers, casino-style games, or dancers adds an extra layer of engagement, keeping guests entertained beyond the dance floor

Although these experiences aren't strictly musical, many of them require a curated soundtrack to enhance the atmosphere. A live painter capturing the event's energy may be accompanied by soft jazz, while a casino-style lounge might be best paired with upbeat swing music to evoke a lively, glamorous feel. Even dancers—whether it's a surprise flash mob or an elegant ballet performance—depend on the perfectly timed soundtrack to bring their art to life.

When thinking about how to enhance your celebration, consider a mix of music and interactive elements to create layered, engaging experiences. These details keep guests entertained throughout the event and ensure that your celebration is vibrant, immersive, and unforgettable.

A well-curated soundtrack flows seamlessly from one moment to the next, enhancing emotions and guiding the energy of the celebration. Whether it's setting the scene for a lively dance party or creating a serene atmosphere for dinner, music is the rhythm of your memories—one that lingers long after the final note.

JACK PAYS 3 TO 2
HIT SOFT
RANCE
Pays 2 to

SETTING THE TONE FOR EVERY MOMENT

Music is the rhythm of any celebration —it sets the mood, guides the flow, and brings people together. Use these notes to create a soundscape that enhances every part of your event:

- **Plan music for every phase:** From guest arrival and cocktails to dinner and dancing, ensure the soundtrack supports each transition with intention.
- **Match the mood:** Choose songs that reflect the energy and emotion you want your guests to feel—elegant, playful, nostalgic, or lively.
- **Be guest-conscious:** Blend personal favorites with crowd-pleasers that resonate across generations and musical tastes.
- **Use professionals for seamless flow:** Consider hiring a DJ, live band, or music director to maintain momentum and adapt to the room's energy.
- **Balance the volume:** Keep it low and conversational during key moments like mingling or dining, then raise the tempo and energy for the dance floor.
- **Think emotional connection:** Select music that not only entertains but tells a story and creates lasting memories.

CHAPTER 10

CAPTURING THE MOMENTS

Documenting Your Celebration Through Videography and Photography.

Often overlooked, videography and photography play a crucial role in capturing the essence of your celebration. Take the time to consider the moments you want to preserve—those beautiful, fleeting details that will be cherished for years to come. Beyond creating memorable experiences, there is nothing more valuable than documenting the emotions, laughter, and special details that make each celebration truly unique.

Reflecting on my own childhood, one thing I wish I had more of are photos and videos that captured those special times. These visuals are not just records; they are treasures that let us relive the warmth of those moments. Moments make memories, and the magic of celebration lies in capturing those fleeting times, so they can be cherished forever. Whether it's capturing the joy of a wedding, the laughter at a milestone birthday, or the intimacy of a family dinner, photography and videography are essential tools for preserving the essence of these occasions.

Documenting Your Celebration Through Videography and Photography

Today, as a planner of celebrations globally, I understand the power of great photography and video. One of my top priorities at every celebration I plan is capturing these priceless memories. For weddings and larger celebrations, I highly recommend investing in professional photographers and filmmakers to preserve the magic of the day. In this chapter, we'll explore how to work with photographers and videographers to ensure that every special moment, from the smallest detail to the grandest gesture, is beautifully captured. I'll share tips on how to highlight key moments and work with professionals to create lasting visual memories.

This chapter explores the art of documenting celebrations, whether through professional lenses or candid smartphone shots. We'll discuss the nuances of both mediums, guide you on when to invest in professionals, and share tips for creating visual stories that last a lifetime.

The Power of Professional Photography

Professional photographers bring expertise, artistry, and an eye for detail that ensures every shot is beautifully composed and thoughtfully edited. For grand occasions like weddings, milestone birthdays, or any event where the details matter, investing in a professional is a no-brainer. The right photographer doesn't just take pictures—they capture energy, emotion, and the soul of a celebration in a way that allows you to relive those moments for years to come.

One of my favorite collaborations in planning events is working with exceptionally talented photographers. Their ability to see and preserve details that others might miss never ceases to amaze me. I've had the privilege of working with some of the best in the industry, capturing both my clients' and my own most cherished moments. There is nothing quite like receiving those first sneak peeks from an event—it feels like reliving the magic all over again. Even after years in the industry, I still find myself in awe of how a single image can transport me right back into the moment.

PHOTOGRAPHY: FREEZING MOMENTS IN TIME

Photography captures the emotions, details, and fleeting expressions that define a celebration, turning them into timeless keepsakes. The cake cutting, the first dance, guests arriving, the special moments and interactions, the intricate table settings—each detail deserves its spotlight. Whether it's a wedding, a milestone birthday, or an intimate gathering, photography serves as the visual storytelling of your event, preserving the magic long after the celebration ends.

WEDDING
First Course
Baby Kale, Shaved Parmesan, Caesar
Second Course
Peekytoe Crab Cake, Celery Root Remoulade,
Dijon Sabayon, Fresh Herb Salad
Entrée
Choice of
Pan Seared Filet Mignon, Short Rib Ragout,
Yukon Potato Puree, Roasted Maitake Mushrooms
Chicken Breast "Coq au Vin", Yukon Potato Puree,
Braised Carrots, Button Mushrooms, Pearl Onions

I asked Amy to share her insights on capturing moments through photography, and she offered these valuable tips:

When working with a photographer for your celebration, communication is key. Share your event timeline in advance and highlight the key moments and special guests you want captured. Don't forget to schedule time for photos of yourself—it's easy to stay busy hosting and miss being in the memories!

Ask your photographer to arrive thirty to sixty minutes early to capture the space and details before guests arrive. Also, be up front about when you'd like the final images delivered and whether you'd prefer to keep the event private or off social media. These simple steps can make a big difference in how your celebration is documented.

One of those incredible talents is Amy Anaiz, an extraordinary photographer and dear friend. Her creativity and attention to detail are unparalleled, and I was thrilled to collaborate with her for this book. The majority of the stunning images featured throughout these pages—the moments, the emotions, the exquisite details—were beautifully captured through her lens.

Capturing Casual Moments: When Your Smartphone Is Enough

Not every celebration requires a professional photographer. For casual gatherings, impromptu get-togethers, or intimate dinners, your smartphone camera can work wonders. With the right lighting, angles, and a bit of creativity, you can still capture stunning memories without a professional budget.

Here are a few quick tips for better smartphone photography:

- **Find the light:** Natural lighting is always best—position subjects near windows or in well-lit areas.
- **Avoid harsh flash:** Instead of using your phone's built-in flash, adjust exposure settings or use nearby lamps or candles for a softer effect.
- **Capture the details:** Don't just take posed group photos—snap pictures of table settings, florals, and handwritten place cards to fully document the experience.

Photography is a way to preserve emotions, relive stories, and capture the fleeting beauty of a moment. Whether through the lens of a professional or the simplicity of your phone, documenting your celebration ensures the joy, laughter, and love shared live on—long after the last toast is made.

INCORPORATING CURATED PHOTO EXPERIENCES GIVES GUESTS A FUN AND ENGAGING WAY TO CAPTURE MEMORIES BEYOND THE STANDARD EVENT PHOTOS.

Creating More Photo Moments: Thoughtful and Stylish Photography Experiences

Photography isn't just about documenting the celebration—it can also be an interactive and stylish part of the event itself. Incorporating curated photo experiences gives guests a fun and engaging way to capture memories beyond the standard event photos.

A fun way to enhance photography at events is by designing a dedicated portrait station—a beautifully styled area where guests can take editorial-style photos. Think of it as a mini photo studio within your celebration, complete with elegant backdrops, floral arrangements, soft lighting, and even a professional photographer or photo concierge to help guests pose effortlessly. These stations elevate the guest experience and ensure they leave with stunning, high quality images.

For a more candid and interactive approach, consider placing Polaroid cameras at designated spots around the venue. Encourage guests to snap impromptu moments throughout the event, capturing the joy and spontaneity of the day. A Polaroid guest book, where attendees can tape their photos and write a message, also makes for a meaningful keepsake.

Whether it's a chic portrait station, a DIY Polaroid corner, or a glam photo booth with customized props, think about how you can incorporate multiple photo moments throughout the celebration. A mix of posed, candid, and interactive elements ensures a versatile and dynamic collection of memories—ones that guests will cherish long after the event is over.

For Stunning Photos

1. Use natural light for a softer, more flattering effect and for evening celebrations, be sure to plan for proper lighting..
2. Frame your shot with intention; pay attention to the background and surroundings.
3. Experiment with candid moments—posed photos are lovely, but unscripted smiles are priceless.
4. Have fun!

VIDEOGRAPHY: TELLING THE STORY

There is a vast difference between videography and photography, and I always emphasize this to my clients—both are equally important in capturing a celebration. While photographs freeze a moment in time, video captures movement, sound, and the true atmosphere of your event.

From the heartfelt welcome moments and emotional speeches to the energy of the dance floor, videography allows you to relive the celebration in its full essence. It brings back not just what you saw, but how it all felt—the laughter, the music, the subtle glances, and all the in-between moments that still images can't fully capture. Whether it's a wedding, milestone birthday, or intimate gathering, investing in a well-crafted event film ensures that the story of your celebration is preserved in a way that feels immersive, cinematic, and timeless.

Highlights and Full Stories

I've had the pleasure of working with some of the most incredibly talented videographers, and their work literally gives me goose bumps. Watching a celebration come to life through video is pure magic—it's a chance to relive the laughter, the emotions, and the energy as if you were experiencing it all over again. Over the years, I have captured countless moments from my personal celebrations, my clients' milestones, and creative projects, and one of the most talented filmmakers I've collaborated with is Kenneth Cooper, who was also behind the scenes for the making of this book.

I asked Kenneth for his insights and tips on videography, and here's what he shared:

As a live event filmmaker, my expertise extends beyond simply capturing moments—I anticipate them. Whether it's a firework grand entrance at a wedding or the quiet smile of a child watching their parents arm in arm, my role is to preserve the essence of these fleeting moments so they can be cherished for generations.

The beauty of a celebration isn't just in the grand, orchestrated moments—it's in the subtle details that often go unnoticed. A couple's hands gently woven together during a speech. A father's proud yet tearful gaze as he watches his daughter dance. A child's quiet wonder as they take in the magic of a family milestone. These are the moments that define a legacy—the ones that time will try to fade but that film has the power to preserve.

For families who deeply value these memories, hiring a professional event filmmaker is more than a practical choice—it's an investment in their legacy. Live event filmmaking requires not just technical skill but a deep understanding of human connection, timing, and storytelling. A great filmmaker is intuitive, collaborative, and attuned to the emotions unfolding in real time, ensuring that nothing is lost in the rush of the day. They allow you to be present in the moment while capturing it for a lifetime.

As a father of two young children, I've come to appreciate how quickly time moves and how precious each moment truly is. Much of my life is spent balancing the present with an awareness of what's to come—living in the now while anticipating the next. That same instinct guides my approach to filmmaking. I strive to be present yet unobtrusive, allowing moments to unfold naturally while ensuring they are beautifully and authentically captured.

Building a relationship with a filmmaker who understands your family, your values, and the significance of your milestones is an essential step in preserving your story. Over time, they won't just document your celebrations; they will become familiar with the people, traditions, and stories that matter most to you. And in doing so, they'll help ensure that the moments you treasure most remain vivid and alive—not just for you, but for generations to come.

WORKING WITH PROFESSIONALS

What to Look For

- **Portfolio:** Review their past work to ensure their style matches your vision.
- **Experience:** Look for professionals who understand the flow of your type of event.
- **Personality:** Your photographer or videographer should make you and your guests feel at ease.

Maximizing Collaboration

- Create a detailed shot list to ensure no moment is missed.
- Share the timeline and any unique moments or surprises in advance.
- Trust their expertise, but don't hesitate to communicate your preferences.

THE BOUJIE WEDDING
PLEASE LEAVE US A MESSAGE
Your Words Mean The World To Us
(1) PICK UP THE PHONE
2) RECORD YOUR VOICEMAIL
3) HANG UP TO ENSURE YOUR
ESSAGE WAS RECORDED
We're so happy you're here!
With love,
The Bouies

SURPRISE ELEMENTS

Curating the guest experience means thinking beyond the expected. Over the years, I've learned that some of the most memorable and emotional moments at celebrations are the surprises—the unexpected gestures that bring an added layer of magic to the event. Whether it's a surprise video message from loved ones, a heartfelt slideshow of memories, an immersive performance, or a grand entertainment reveal, these moments evoke pure joy and connection.

Planning ahead is key to ensuring these surprises are not only well executed but also beautifully captured on video. If you're hosting at home or at an intimate gathering without a professional videographer, be intentional about how you'll document these moments—whether it's designating a trusted friend to film on a high-quality phone or setting up a discreet camera in the right location.

Tips for Seamless Ambiance

Ambiance and music play a crucial role in shaping the atmosphere of your celebration, influencing not just the guest experience but also how moments are captured in photos and videos. Thoughtfully selected music enhances emotional depth, setting the perfect backdrop for visual storytelling. From warm, welcoming melodies as guests arrive to the lively beats that fill the dance floor, a seamless musical flow ensures that every captured image and video reflects the energy and essence of your event.

Aligning music choices with each phase of the celebration helps create cohesion between sound, visuals, and emotions, allowing your event's story to unfold naturally. The right soundtrack doesn't just complement the moment—it enhances the way it is remembered through photography and videography.

Photography and videography are the threads that weave the story of your celebration. By intentionally planning how to document your events—whether through professional lenses or personal snapshots—you create a lasting tapestry of memories to cherish forever.

For larger celebrations, hiring a professional videographer ensures that these surprise elements are captured with the emotion and artistry they deserve. Be sure to discuss any planned surprises in advance with your videographer so they can be positioned to capture the reactions authentically. A great filmmaker doesn't just document—they anticipate. Share with them the significance of these moments, whether it's an unexpected dance performance, a touching video montage, or a grand fireworks reveal, so they can capture the emotions, reactions, and energy in a way that feels immersive and true to the experience.

Some of my favorite memories from celebrations I've planned have come from these surprise elements—the pure joy on a bride's face when she sees a surprise guest flown in, the overwhelming emotions of a heartfelt video message, or the collective awe of guests when an unexpected performance begins. It's in these moments that celebrations become more than just events—they become deeply personal experiences that guests will never forget.

PRESERVING THE BEAUTY OF THE DAY

Your celebration deserves to be remembered just as beautifully as it was experienced. Use this guide to ensure your memories are thoughtfully and meaningfully captured:

- **Plan ahead:** Communicate your vision clearly with your photographer or videographer so they understand your style and priorities.
- **Create a shot list:** Identify key people, details, and moments that must be captured—from decor and guest arrivals to special rituals and candid joy.
- **Hire or DIY?** Decide if you'll bring in a professional team or opt for a more personal, behind-the-scenes approach.
- **Invite guest contributions:** Encourage guests to share their own photos and videos for additional perspectives and fun, behind-the-scenes memories.
- **Prioritize candidness:** Some of the most meaningful images are unplanned—let natural emotions and interactions unfold.
- **Mix mediums:** Blend still photography and video for a richer storytelling experience.
- **Back it up:** Protect your memories by saving all photos and videos in multiple secure locations—digital and physical.

Final Thoughts

Celebrations are the stories we tell, the connections we nurture, and the love we share. My hope is that this book has left you feeling inspired, empowered, and excited to create your own meaningful moments, whether through a beautifully set table, a thoughtful menu, or simply the joy of bringing people together in an unforgettable way.

The Art of Celebrating is not just a guide to hosting and entertaining; it's a reflection of the lessons I've learned, the experiences I've cherished, and the traditions that have shaped me. From my childhood in Nigeria, where celebrations were woven into everyday life, to planning events around the world, I've come to understand that at the heart of every gathering—big or small—is the opportunity to honor life's beauty and the people we hold dear.

As you embark on your own journey of celebrating, remember that it's not about perfection—it's about intention. It's about crafting spaces where love is felt, laughter is shared, and memories are made. Whether you're planning a grand wedding, an intimate dinner, or a casual gathering with friends, the magic lies in the thoughtfulness and care you put into each detail. The best celebrations are the ones that make people feel seen, valued, and connected.

Thank you for allowing me to share my stories, my tips, and my heart with you. I hope this book becomes a companion you return to, not just for ideas, but as a reminder of the power of celebrating with joy, creativity, and love. Here's to many beautiful celebrations ahead—may they be filled with meaning, connection, and magic.

ACKNOWLEDGMENTS

First and foremost, I give thanks to God for the gifts He has blessed me with and for guiding my unique path to this moment. Every step, every lesson, and every opportunity has been part of His divine plan, and I am forever grateful for the grace and favor that have brought me here.

To my husband, Akin—my rock, my greatest supporter, and the love of my life. Your unwavering belief in me, your patience through the long nights, and your endless encouragement mean the world to me. This journey would not be possible without you.

To my incredible team—Merlyn, Imani, Frediliza, Lin, Diane, Assumpta, and every member of the Kesh Events family over the past decade, whether in planning, design, or production. You have been there through the highs and the lows, pouring your heart into every event, every detail, and every celebration. The intensity of our productions, the magic we create, and the memories we share are what make this journey so fulfilling. I could not do this without you, and I am forever grateful for your dedication and talent.

A special thank you to the creative team that was knee-deep in the book production and shoot. To Amy Anaiz, the visionary photographer behind the breathtaking images in this book—your artistry and passion are unmatched. To Kenneth Cooper, for capturing the essence of this journey through film and behind-the-scenes magic. To Delma at Tailored Elements, for the exquisite custom linens that added beauty and texture to these pages. Your talent and hard work brought this vision to life in ways I could only dream of.

To Dami Okuboyejo of By Dami Studios—thank you for your sisterhood, your friendship, and the heart you poured into every page of this book. Your artistry and thoughtful design brought *The Art of Celebrating* to life in the most beautiful way. Every detail reflects your care, talent, and the deep intention behind your work. I am immensely grateful for your brilliance, your belief in this project, and for walking this journey with me.

To our amazing clients—you have not only seen my work, but you have trusted me with your most cherished celebrations. I am honored to be part of your stories, and I hold your trust and love in a special place in my heart.

To the incredible creatives I collaborate with year after year—photographers, floral designers, cake artists, venue teams, stationery designers, and every vendor who contributes to the magic of these events—thank you. Your artistry, professionalism, and dedication inspire me every single day.

To Rebecca Grinnals and Kathryn Arce of Engage! Summits—thank you for your friendship, your support, and for so graciously writing the foreword for this book. The platform and community you've built have been a source of inspiration and connection, and I am deeply grateful for the opportunities Engage! has brought into my life.

To the Greenleaf Books team—thank you for believing in me and my vision for this book, and for helping bring it to life and share it with the world. From the editorial team to consulting, management, and beyond, I am truly appreciative of your hard work and guidance.

To the creatives and clients featured in this book—thank you for your trust, collaboration, and support. This book would not have been possible without you. Your celebrations and creativity have inspired me in ways beyond words.

To the media, conferences, speaking engagements, TV features, and blogs that have shared my journey and given me a platform to inspire and teach—thank you for seeing me and sharing my voice with the world.

To my circle of friends—you ride for me, support me, and cheer for me every single day. I feel your love, and I love you right back. Thank you for being my people.

And finally, to my family—thank you for your endless love and support. I am grateful for the gift of family and cherish each and every one of you.

This book is a labor of love, a reflection of years of passion, hard work, and an unshakable belief in the beauty of celebrating life. To everyone who has been part of this journey, thank you from the depths of my heart. xx

PHOTOGRAPHY CREDITS

The cover and some of the photography featured throughout this book were captured by Amy Anaiz (amyanaiz.com). Her creative vision and exceptional talent helped bring *The Art of Celebrating* to life in the most beautiful way.

We are also grateful to the following photographers who contributed their stunning work to this book. Each image helped tell the story of celebration, style, and meaningful connection.

Thank you all for your artistry and contribution.

Featured Photographers:

Amy Anaiz Photography (amyanaiz.com)
Chapters: Cover, 1, 2, 3, 4, 5, 6, 7, 8, 9, 10
Cover photo
Pages: v, x, xii, 3, 5 (bottom), 8, 9, 14, 15, 17, 24, 25, 26, 27, 31, 33, 34, 36, 39 (left), 49, 58, 62, 67, 76, 78, 85, 87, 90, 93 (right), 95 (top left), 95 (top right), 96, 97, 98, 95 (top right), 112 (bottom), 114, 115 (left), 117, 119 (top left), 124, 128–149, 154, 156, 157, 161 (top), 152, 163, 164, 165 (bottom), 167, 168, 169, 170, 171, 173, 174, 175 (bottom), 178, 179, 182, 183 (top), 185 (top left), 188, 190, 191, 193, 194, 195, 196, 197, 199, 200, 201, 202, 203, 204, 205, 206, 207, 208, 209, 213, 214, 216, 217, 211, 226, 227, 229, 230, 231 (top), 238, 242, 243, 247, 251 (top), 252, 256, 270, 272, 273, 276, 278, 279, 290, 291, 296, 306

Collin Pierson Photography (collinpierson.com)
Chapters: 1, 2, 3, 4, 6, 7, 8, 10
Pages: ii, viii, 5 (top), 10, 11, 16, 39 (right), 47 (bottom), 100, 102, 103, 104, 105, 116, 121 (right), 125 (bottom), 155 (bottom), 183 (bottom), 185 (top right), 233, 237, 289 (bottom), 241, 244, 245, 246, 281 (top)

Lucy Munoz Photography (lucymunozphotography.com)
Chapters: 1, 2, 3, 4, 6, 7, 8, 9, 10
Pages: 6, 12, 13, 22, 23, 30, 41, 42, 44, 46, 48, 54, 55, 61 (left), 63, 64, 65, 71 (left), 74, 81, 90, 106, 107, 112 (top), 115 (right), 120, 125 (left), 126, 127 (top), 152, 153 (bottom), 158, 189 (top right and left), 223, 224, 225, 254, 257 (top left, top, bottom left, bottom right), 258, 259 (bottom), 260, 274, 275, 288, 294, 295 (bottom)

Rudney Novaes Photography (rudneynovaes.com)
Chapters: 1, 2, 3, 4, 6, 7, 8, 9, 10
Pages: vi, 4, 45, 53, 56, 57 (bottom left & bottom right), 59 (left), 61 (right), 68, 70, 71 (right), 72 (bottom), 73, 75, 80, 86, 95 (bottom left), 108, 109, 110, 122, 150, 153 (top), 160, 175 (top), 177, 189 (bottom left), 192 (top), 210, 211, 250, 257 (top right), 259 (top), 297

Mack Julion Photography (mackjulion.com)
Chapters: 1, 2, 9
Pages: 18, 19, 57 (top left), 69, 263

Syed Yaqeen Photography (syedyaqeen.com)
Chapters: 1, 2, 7, 8
Pages: 20, 21, 47 (top), 218

Koman Photography (komanphotography.com)
Chapter: 1
Pages: 28, 29

Hannah Schweiss Photography
Chapters: 1, 3, 6, 8, 9, 10
Pages: 38, 40, 51, 91, 155 (top), 166, 180, 185, 228, 234, 235, 248, 251 (bottom), 264, 277, 280, 283, 284, 286, 289, 293, 305

Nicee Martin
Chapters: 2, 3, 4, 6, 10
Pages: 50, 57 (top right), 60, 119 (top right, bottom left, bottom right), 185 (bottom left), 295 (top)

Candace Sims Photography (candacesimsphotography.com)
Chapters: 2, 3, 6, 7, 8
Pages: 59 (right), 88, 89, 99, 181, 231 (bottom), 289 (top)

Zazu Productions
Chapter: 2
Page: 72 (top)

Reem Photography (reemphotography.com)
Chapters: 3, 6, 7, 10
Pages: 79(top), 84, 165 (top), 172, 192 (bottom), 241 (top), 281 (bottom)

Carasco Photography (carascophoto.com)
Chapters: 3, 4
Pages: 79, 111, 113, 125 (bottom), 241 (bottom)

Vito Radé Photography
Chapters: 3, 6,9
Pages: 92, 185 (bottom right), 268

Susie and Will Photography (susieandwill.com)
Chapters: 3, 4,6
Pages: 93 (left), 112 (bottom), 161 (bottom)

Guri Gashi Photography
Chapters: 6, 9
ages: 159, 265, 266, 267, 269

Dmitry Shumanev Photography (dmitryshumanev.com)
Chapters: 7, 8, 10
ages: 186, 189 (bottom right), 232 (left), 240, 292

Lacour Images (lacourimages.com)
Chapter: 8
Page: 232 (left)

Kendall Lauren Photography (kendalllaurenphotography.com)
Chapter: 8
Page: 253

RESOURCES & CREDITS

Creating this book was a collaborative effort, and I am deeply grateful for the incredible talents, insights, and contributions that helped bring *The Art of Celebrating* to life. From expert interviews and creative collaborations to the photographers and designers who helped visually capture the essence of each chapter, this book is a reflection of many hands and hearts working together.

This section acknowledges and credits the amazing individuals and teams who played a role in shaping the content, visuals, and inspiration throughout these pages.Each chapter is a testament to the artistry, knowledge, and passion of those who have dedicated their craft to celebrating life's most meaningful moments. A heartfelt thank you to everyone who contributed their expertise, creativity, and support—you are an invaluable part of this journey.

COVER SHOOT

Photography: Amy Anaiz, **Linens**: Tailored Elements, **Candles**: Ozaiz Home, **Menus**: By Dami Studios

CHAPTER 1: INSPIRATION – SETTING THE FOUNDATION FOR YOUR CELEBRATION

Photography: Amy Anaiz, Collin Pierson, Rudney Novaes, Lucy Munoz, Mack Julion, Syed Raqeen, Koman Photography, Hannah Schweiss

Menus & Stationery: By Dami Studios – pages 10, 20, 24–25, 38, 41, 42,

Linens, Draping & Details: Tailored Elements (Linens & Chair Caps) – pages 24–25, Nuage Designs – page 34–35, Art of Imagination (Draping & Lighting) – page 34–35

Candles: Ozaiz Home – pages 26, 31,33

Venues & Locations: Château De Villette, France – pages 11, 22–23, 29, NIZUC Resort, Mexico – pages 32–33, Lake Como, Italy – pages 42–43, Waldorf Astoria, Chicago – page 50, The Langham Hotel, Chicago – pages 14 15, 17, Chez – pages 20–21

Catering: Entertaining Company - page 17

Entertainment & Music: Jazz Around Midnight – page 28, Maria Gallo Productions – pages 18-19, 32–33

Additional Features: Vague (Classic Car) – page 29

CHAPTER 2: CREATING MEMORABLE MOMENTS: ADDING PERSONAL TOUCHES

Photography: Amy Anaiz, Collin Pierson, Rudney Novaes, Lucy Munoz, Mack Julion, Nicee Martin

Menus & Stationery: By Dami Studios – pages , 46–47, 50–51,55, 59–62, 65–66, Ceci New York (Menu Design) – pages 45,53, 56, 59, 61, 68, Adorn Unlimited (Embroidered Napkins) – page 50

Linens, Draping & Details: Tailored Elements (Custom Napkins) – pages 44, 62

Venues & Locations: The Langham, Chicago – pages 49, 54–55, Oheka Castle, New York – page 45, 53, Château De Villette, France – pages 48, 71, 74, Shangri-La, Paris – pages 63–65

Entertainment & Music: Jazz Around Midnight – pages 48,61–65, Spark Entertainment Group – page 49

Additional Features: Chef Daniel (Cake) – page 63, Fêtes & Feux (Fireworks, Château De Villette) – page 74

CHAPTER 3: INVITATIONS: CREATING THE PERFECT FIRST IMPRESSION

Photography: Amy Anaiz, Rudney Novaes, Lucy Munoz, Nicee Martin, Candace Sims, Reem Photography, Carasco Photography, Vito Rade, Hannah Schweiss, Susie and Will

Invitations & Stationery: By Dami Studios – pages 76, 79, 83–85, 87, 90–91, 93, 95–98, 172, Elizabeth Grace – page 79,83, Ceci New York – pages 78, 86, 95, Ooh Aah Invitations – pages 88–89, 99

CHAPTER 4: MENU PLANNING: A CULINARY EXPERIENCE.

Photography: Amy Anaiz, Collin Pierson, Nicee Martin, Carasco Photography, Susie and Will, Lucy Munoz Photography, Rudney Novaes,

Catering, Venue & Culinary Features: Page 106: Mini Cakes – Vanille Patisserie, Page 101: Catering – Entertaining Company: Pages 100, 103, 105,: Catering & Venue – Shangri-La, Paris, Page 106: Catering & Venue – Monsieur Bleu, Pages 108–110: Catering & Venue – Gansevoort, NYC Meatpacking, Page 111: Seafood Station & Venue – The Drake Hotel, Chicago, Page 112: Catering & Venue – The Langham, Chicago; Mini Cake – Pistores, Page 113: Passed Desserts – The Drake Hotel, Chicago, Pages 114–115: Catering – The Langham, Chicago, Pages 116: Signature Drinks – Entertaining Company, Pages 118–121: Stationery – By Dami Studios, Page 127: Catering – The Drake Hotel & Shangri-La, Paris, Page 127: Cake – Toni Patisserie; Mini Cakes – Vanille Patisserie

CHAPTER 5: COOKING: PARTY FAVORITES FROM MY NIGERIAN CHILDHOOD.

Photography: Amy Anaiz

CHAPTER 6: SIGNATURE DRINKS: TOASTING TO THE OCCASION.

Photography: Amy Anaiz, Rudney Novaes, Lucy Munoz, Hannah Schweiss, Nicee Martin, Candace Sims, Reem Photography, Vito Rade, Guri Gashi

Creative Partners & Features: Pages 158, 167: Custom Ice Cubes – Johnson Studios Ice Sculpture, Page 159: Signature Drinks & Venue – Beatnik on the River, Page 161: Signature Drinks & Venue – The Langham, Chicago, Page 156: Glassware – Ozaiz Home, Page 178: Cocktail Napkins – My Drap, Pages 157,161, 164, 184–185: Stationery – By Dami Studios

CHAPTER 7: FLORAL DESIGN: SETTING THE MOOD WITH FLOWERS.

Photography: Amy Anaiz, Collin Pierson, Hannah Schweiss, Reem Photography, Dmitry Shumanev, Lucy Munoz Photography, Reem Photography

Creative Partners: : Pages 186–189: San Francisco City Hall, Pages 189, 192, 210–211, : Location – Oheka Castle, Pages 193, 205, 209, 215 Linens – Tailored Elements, Candles – Ozaiz Home, Menus – By Dami Studios

CHAPTER 8: TABLE SETTING: DESIGNING A BEAUTIFUL TABLESCAPE.

Photography: Amy Anaiz, Collin Pierson, Syed Raqeen, Lucy Munoz, Hannah Schweiss, Candace Sims, Lacour Images, Kendall Lauren Photography, Dmitry Shumanev

Menus & Stationery: By Dami Studios – pages 224–228, 243–247, Gourmet Invitations – pages 219, 241, Elizabeth Grace – page 232, Ooh Aah Invitations – page 239

Linens & Details: Tailored Elements – pages 214–216, 221, 226–227, 230–231, 243, 247, 251, Lola Valentina Design (Custom Charger Plates & Napkins) – page 223, Windy City Linen – pages 239–241

Candles & Lighting: Ozaiz Home – pages 214, 215, 222–223, 237, A Posh Production (Lighting) – pages 239–241, 247, Tables, Chairs & Rentals:, Elle and Rose – pages 227, 239–241

Venues & Locations: San Francisco City Hall – pages 232, 240, Charcoal Factory – pages 233, 236–237, 244–246, Morgan Manufacturing – page 253, The langham Hotel, Chicago – page 248

Catering: Entertaining Company – page 253

CHAPTER 9: MUSIC: SETTING THE TONE FOR THE CELEBRATION.

Photography: Amy Anaiz, Rudney Novaes, Lucy Munoz, Mack Julion, Hannah Schweiss, Guri Gashi, Vito Rade
Entertainment & Music: Gold Coast All Stars – page 256, Jazz Around Midnight – pages 254, 257, 259, Mylez Gittens – pages 257, 259, Beatmix Music – pages 258, 264–269, Maria Gallo Productions – pages 263, DJ Megan Taylor – page 267, 269
Special Effects: Fêtes & Feux (Fireworks) – page 260

CHAPTER 10: CAPTURING THE MOMENTS: VIDEO AND PHOTOGRAPHY

Photography: Amy Anaiz, Collin Pierson, Lucy Munoz, Hannah Schweiss, Nicee Martin, Reem Photography, Dmitry Shumanev
Creative Details & Design: Custom Napkins: Tailored Elements – page 289, 293, 295, Menus & Signage: By Dami Studios – pages 272,273,274,277,278, 289,290, 293, 295, Venue: The Langham, Chicago – pages 270–276, 278–279, Bian: 280, Charcoal Factory – 280, The Waldorf, Chicago – 286, Chairs: Ellie and Rose – page 274, 288, Linens & Chargers: Lola Valentina Design – page 274, Draping & Lighting: A Posh Production – page 274, Mini Cakes & Cake: Pistores – pages 275–276
Entertainment & Music: Spark Entertainment Group – page 293, Beatmix Music – page 294, Fireworks: Grucci – page 297

ABOUT THE AUTHOR

Akeshi Akinseye is a leading voice in luxury event planning and design, celebrated for her ability to curate sophisticated, one-of-a-kind celebrations that blend artistry, storytelling, and meticulous attention to detail. As the visionary behind Kesh Events, a global luxury planning and design firm, and *The Art of Celebrating* blog and magazine, Akeshi has spent over a decade orchestrating tailor-made weddings, milestone events, and experiences for discerning clients across the world. Her signature style and dedication to creating intentional, unforgettable moments have made her one of the most sought-after event planners in the industry.

Akeshi's passion for celebrating life's most meaningful moments was instilled in her from childhood. Growing up in Benin City, Nigeria, she was immersed in a world where hospitality and celebrations were a way of life. Her mother, a talented hostess and entrepreneur in party planning, baking, and hospitality, was her greatest influence. Inspired by her mother's effortless ability to create joyful gatherings, Akeshi developed a deep appreciation for design, entertainment, and the art of bringing people together. From an early age, she was already exploring her creative talents—baking, cooking, sewing, and designing—all of which became the foundation for her celebrated career in event planning, design, and lifestyle.

Today, Akeshi is internationally recognized for her exceptional work and has been featured in leading publications such as *Forbes, People, Architectural Digest, Elle Decor, Brides, Munaluchi Bride, Essence, Condé Nast Traveler, New York Times*, and more. She has earned numerous accolades, including being named *one of the best wedding planners in America* by Brides and *top planner* by PartySlate.

Akeshi's philosophy is simple yet profound: Every celebration should tell a story—one that is personal, intentional, and unforgettable. Her approach to event planning goes beyond aesthetics; she curates experiences that capture emotion, reflect her clients' unique stories, and create lasting memories. Through Kesh Events, she has built a reputation for producing celebrations that are visually stunning yet deeply meaningful, seamlessly blending beauty, culture, and creativity.

Beyond event production, Akeshi is a best-selling author and the host of *The Art of Celebrating* podcast, where she shares her expertise and passion for elevating life's special moments. Her books, courses, and mentorship programs have empowered countless creatives and hosts to embrace the art of celebration, offering expert guidance and inspiration for creating stylish, meaningful events.

Whether she's designing a grand wedding, producing an intimate gathering, speaking on global platforms, or sharing her insights through writing and mentorship, Akeshi's dedication to her craft remains unwavering. She continues to push the boundaries of creativity and event design, inspiring others to elevate every moment into an extraordinary experience.

Join Akeshi on her journey to transform celebrations into an art form, and let her guide you in creating experiences that are timeless, luxurious, and deeply personal.

Follow along:
Websites: ***akeshiakinseye.com, keshevents.com, and theartofcelebrating.com***
Instagram: ***@akeshiakinseye, @keshevents, and @taoclifestyle***